I0880227

"The Greatest

Battle of the Age"

New Yorkers at First Bull Run

R.L. Murray

I.S.B.N. 0-9659177-4-6

Benedum Books

13205 Younglove Road
Wolcott, NY 14590

For a complete list of titles see

www.nyincivilwar.com

This book is dedicated to

the Volunteer and Professional

Firefighters in

New York City

and

New York State.

In appreciation of your faithful service

to your communities

and your country during times

of peace and war.

God bless you all.

And in Memory of the Firemen
who fell in the line of duty at
First Bull Run and
September 11, 2001.

Table of Contents

<u>Acknowledgments</u>

I would like to take this opportunity to thank the people who helped make this work possible. A special thanks to my wife, Tammany, who helped with this project and especially took a leading role in typing the letters for the companion book, *Letters from the Front: First Bull Run.*

Great appreciation to Ron Patrick for editing and to my brother, William Murray, for making available some research materials that were very valuable to the project. Bill also helped rekindle my interest in the Civil War many years ago.

Also thanks to Rebekah Ambrose, Sue Ayers, Joseph Bilby, Amy Castor, Dixie Castor, Jessie Compton, Nancy Compton, Deborah Ferrell, Bob Huddleston, Joseph Luciano, Patricia Luciano, Cathy Mulford, Ruth Rosenberg-Naparsteck, Karen Osborn, Ann Salter and Ann Walton for research assistance.

Thank you also to the following institutions:

Cayuga Community College Library
Clyde Savannah Public Library
Cornell University Library
Geneseo State Library
Geneva Historical Society
Milne Library, Oneonta State
Onondaga County Historical Society
Rochester Historian's Office
Rochester Historical Society
Rundell Library (Rochester, N.Y.)
Saint Lawrence University Library
Seymour Library (Auburn, N.Y.)
University of Rochester Library
Wayne County Historian's Office

Introduction

A historical account of New Yorkers' participation in the Battle at First Bull Run has been long overdue. The battle itself has been a fairly neglected topic, mainly because it was quickly eclipsed by larger encounters as the war progressed. Although this battle was relatively small, compared to later struggles, to that point in American history it was, as one soldier stated in a letter home, "*The Greatest Battle of the Age.*"[1]

When beginning this study I was very pleasantly surprised by the amount of primary sources found, nearly two hundred letters written by soldiers during this period. The information they provided was so interesting and extensive we not only used them in this history, but also compiled many of these writings into a companion letter book.

The events in this work, from the men volunteering after Fort Sumter to the Battle at Bull Run on July 21, 1861, are depicted as much as possible through the soldiers' own words. Nearly every page contains extensive quotes from these witnesses. In fact, well over half of the works cited are letters written by the men that have never been utilized by other historians. Their writings shed new light on the events and provide details that were until now unknown.

Although these primary sources provided wonderful personal interest stories and new perspectives on the events, they also created some problems; many times men in the same unit give conflicting accounts, making it difficult to understand what was happening. Two factors contributed to this as compared to writings in later battles. First, few of these men had ever experienced combat before; thus the excitement and "fog of battle" clouded how they remembered the events. Second, these regiments were very large, numbering from 600 to 800 men, with some over a 1,000. These commands were two or three times the size of regiments in later battles, such as Gettysburg, where many Union regiments were smaller than 250 men (ranks were thinned by previous casualties and disease). Thus, while a man at one end of the regiment was experiencing one thing, someone on the other end of the line could have been experiencing something com-

---

[1] J.D.M. letter.

pletely different. Additionally, if one end of the line experienced heavy fire, while the other was protected or out of range, some men would write about this action, while others might not even mention anything concerning this phase of the battle. This also explains how a man could write, for example, how their line came to rest on a hill, while another recalled they were in a valley. If their regimental formation stretched across the elevation and into the valley, this would make perfect sense.

The reader must also keep another factor in mind when reading this work. This is not a history of the Battle of Bull Run, but rather a history of New Yorkers' participation in the battle. Thus, details such as the specific shifting and placement of Confederate troops, listing times and regimental units and commanders' names, and stories such as how "Stonewall" Jackson got his name are not included in the text. While these are important details for a study of the campaign, they could easily distract from our focus – New Yorkers' role in the battle.

Additionally, some New York units receive more attention than others. The key factor influencing this was the availability of primary and secondary sources. Some units had regimental histories while others did not. Some units, mainly the upstate regiments, had an abundance of primary sources available through letters reprinted (and fortunately preserved) in their local newspapers. Unfortunately, this practice was not commonplace in New York City papers. Thus, the more information available, the more we had to share. Another note about units covered; the scope of this study was on those New York commands that crossed Bull Run and became engaged in the battle, not on those that remained in reserve on the other side of the creek, even if they were involved in the retreat to Washington.

Once again, we would like to take this opportunity to thank all of you, the readers. Your continued support for these projects allows us to further our research. Our goal here at *Benedum Books* is to document the efforts of New Yorkers in the Civil War, allowing their stories to be told.

R.L. Murray
Wolcott, N.Y.
April, 2002

Chapter One

"God and Our Native Land!"

Well, the long suspense is at an end. The Jeff. Davis Rebels have begun a Civil War of which no man can foretell the duration or its result....[1]

The attack on Fort Sumter on April 12, 1861, was a dramatic call to arms for the Northern population. When President Lincoln issued his first appeal for troops, 75,000 militia from the states, "to maintain the honor, the integrity and the existence of our National Union...", the response was overwhelming. New York's Legislature authorized thirty-eight regiments to take the field.[2]

Lincoln's call was for immediate help, troops needed to defend the Capital. Thus, he requested the governors to mobilize their militia units. Men from New York quickly joined regiments, both existing militia commands – mainly from New York City – and some newly forming volunteer units. These men would sign on for ninety days of Federal service and two additional years of state duty – presumably, to be served within New York State.[3]

---

[1] Rochester *Union and Advertiser*, April 13, 1861.

[2] James McPherson, *Battle Cry of Freedom*, (Oxford University Press: 1988), 274; *Lyons Republican*, April 19, 1861; Allan Nevins, *The War For the Union: The Improvised War.* (New York: 1959), 78 and 175. War Department fixed state quotas: New York, heading the list as the most populous state, would provide 17 regiments, Pennsylvania 16, Ohio 13, Illinois 6, and the remaining one or two each.

[3] Nevins, *The Improvised War*, 78 and 88; Cazeau, *Account of the Thirteenth New York*, 2; Ensign Gilbert letter, July 27, 1861.

Civilian response in the Empire State was also impressive. War committees organized and patriotic meetings were held, calling for volunteers and money to support the government. The largest and most influential organization in the state was the Union Defense Committee in New York City. This group played an important role in the first months of the war, both unifying efforts behind the Federal cause and providing valuable funds – actually paying for arms, equipment and transportation for the first units bound for Washington. They also encouraged enlistments by promising to help the soldiers' families financially.[4]

In the upstate communities, funds were also established and meetings held. In Rochester, citizens pledged over $28,000 "to support the families who have, and who wish to volunteer in support of our country's right and honor." The committee did much to unify the community, calling for citizens to put aside their political differences, asking "whether Democrat or Republican, to forget his political party and prejudice, and to unite as true born and loyal Americans in supporting the 'Stars and Stripes.'"[5]

Political unity and patriotism were two significant responses to the attack on Fort Sumter, even from those previously holding pro-Southern points of view. "The change in public sentiment here is wonderful – almost miraculous," wrote a New York City merchant after Fort Sumter.[6] Incredibly, much talk in the city previous to the attack was blatantly in opposition to the Union. One prominent newspaper headline read: "The City of New York belongs almost as much to the South as to the North." Mayor Fernando Wood had even openly talked of New York City breaking away, making itself independent.[7] Fortunately, Sumter quieted such talk,

---

[4] Ernest A. McKay, *The Civil War and New York City* (Syracuse University Press: 1990), 79. Immediately after Fort Sumter, New York City's common council authorized a million dollars to equip regiments and another half million to provide for the families of the soldiers. Nevins, *The Improvised War*, 88.

[5] "Rochester for the Union!" Rochester *Union and Advertiser*, April 17, 1861; Rochester *Democrat and American*, April 24 and 25, 1861.

[6] Quoted in McPherson, *Battle Cry of Freedom*, 274.

[7] From a New York City newspaper, the *Evening Post*. Quoted in McKay, *The Civil War and New York City*, 18 and 56-58. Much of New York, both banking and trade, had close ties to the Southern economy.

and now sentiment continued to grow in favor of preserving the Union.

On April 20, 1861, a dramatic demonstration showing the reversal of public opinion was held in Union Square. Thousands of New Yorkers rallied at what was called "the largest meeting ever held on this continent," to show their support not only for the Union, but also the commander of Fort Sumter, Major Robert Anderson, and the men that served under him.[8]

Thousands of would-be volunteers flocked to recruiting offices, hoping to sign their names on the muster rolls. In New York City, most enlistees joined the ranks of already existing militia units. On paper these commands would number 780 officers and men at full strength, but in the years preceding the war, most of the ranks diminished to less than half that number. In reality, the functional capability of most militia units was limited to performing ceremonial duties such as firing guns on the Fourth of July and marching in parades.[9] Now, new men joined and older members resigned. These units prepared to go to war.

Among the militia regiments, the most famous, or at least notorious, was the 69th New York State Militia. This command was almost exclusively Irishmen and had recently fallen into disfavor with both the city and higher governmental authorities. An incident occurred during a recent visit to the United States by the Prince of Wales. In recognition of such an important figure, the city planned a precession and celebration. In conjunction with this, the 69th New York was expected to march and pay tribute to the foreign dignitary. For the Irishmen, however, this was an unacceptable request. Colonel Michael Corcoran, the commander of the 69th, stated they could not honor "a sovereign, under whose rule Ireland was left a desert and her best sons exiled or banished,"

The prospect of debts being cancelled and future trade being reduced was decidedly unappealing to many New York City residents.

[8] Thomas S. Townsend, *Honors of the Empire State in the War of the Rebellion* (New York: 1889), 34; Nevins, *The Improvised War*, 76; McKay, *The Civil War and New York City*, 62 – 63.

[9] Nevins, *The Improvised War*, 78; McPherson, *Battle Cry of Freedom*, 317.

and the 69th refused to march. The militia command was then stripped of her colors and Corcoran brought up on charges.[10]

With the new national emergency, this incident lost much of its sting. Rumors now spread through the city, however, that the 69th planned to sail south and offer its services to the Confederacy. Thus, when the Irish community and members of the 69th instead vocally came out in support of the Union, not only was the city relieved but Colonel Corcoran was restored to command and their colors returned. With this, recruits for the 69th came pouring in.[11]

While the 69th and the other city militia units were still organizing, the 6th Massachusetts paraded through New York's streets. Governor John Andrew of Massachusetts, through valuable foresight, previously saw to it that his state militia was well equipped and ready for just such an emergency. The day after the president's call, his first regiment, the 6th Massachusetts, set out for Washington. On the 17th they passed through New York, by rail, eating breakfast in the city. Afterwards, they marched down Broadway amidst cheering crowds and boarded trains for the Capital. Seeing these well-dressed and drilled troops greatly inspired the New Yorkers. In just two more days one of their finest units would also parade off to war.[12]

The first command to head south was the 7th New York State Militia, the "darling Seventh," made up predominantly of members of New York City's high society. On April 19, 1861, they marched down the streets in their militia gray uniforms with white belts and set out on their journey with sandwiches made at Delmonico's and one thousand velvet covered campstools – presumably to sit and eat their sandwiches on. Although the president's call had been for ninety-day enlistments, these troops only agreed to serve thirty days. But, in the emergency, their offer was accepted. The "darling Seventh" marched proudly down Broadway with two additional Massachusetts regiments that had just arrived.

---

[10] D. P. Conyngham, *The Irish Brigade and Its Campaigns.* (New York: 1867), 19-20 and 537.

[11] McKay, *The Civil War and New York City*, 57 and 61-62; Conyngham, *The Irish Brigade*, 27 and 537.

[12] Nevins, *The Improvised War*, 79 – 80.

The 7th New York Militia marching off to Washington.

Together they began their journey with a tremendous sendoff from a roaring crowd.[13]

In Washington, the situation was growing increasingly more dangerous. The presence of Union troops was desperately needed. Much instability existed in neighboring Maryland, especially in Baltimore; no one knew if the state would secede and troops would march on the Capital. On the same day the 7th paraded down Broadway in New York, the 6th Massachusetts was passing through Baltimore. As the troops disembarked from their cars to march across town to catch another train, an angry crowd gathered. A shot rang out while the soldiers passed through the mob, and within minutes four soldiers lay dead, along with a larger number of civilians. The 6th was soon loaded on cars and headed for Washington. Baltimore, however, was in turmoil. Soon the bridges to the city were destroyed, cutting the primary land route to the nation's capital.[14]

With rail transportation disrupted, the situation in Washington grew more desperate. Not only would troops headed south need to find an alternate route, but another method for sending supplies to the city was needed. At this point, a well-known upstate New York lawyer, landowner and philanthropist, named James Wadsworth, took it upon himself to charter two vessels and load them with supplies at his own expense. Wadsworth accompanied the ships south, traveling first to Annapolis, Maryland, then proceeding by land to Washington.

Before the war, James Wadsworth was an outspoken anti-slavery man. At the outbreak of hostilities he traveled to Albany, volunteering his services to Governor Morgan, from whom he received a commission. Thus, Major James Wadsworth made him-

---

[13] McKay, *The Civil War and New York City*, 67 – 68; Geoffrey C. Ward, *The Civil War: An Illustrated History*. (New York: 1990), 49 – 50; Nevins, *The Improvised War*, 86; William Todd, *The Seventy-Ninth Highlanders: New York Volunteers in the War of Rebellion*. (Albany, N.Y.: 1886), 2.

[14] Nevins, *The Improvised War*, 77 and 81 – 82.

Major James Wadsworth on General McDowell's staff.
Wadsworth is pictured here as a brigadier general.
He was killed while leading troops forward
during the Battle of the Wilderness in 1864.

Miller's Photographic History of the Civil War

self and tons of welcome supplies available to the Federal government during this time of crisis.[15]

Back in New York City, more regiments were prepared to leave. The 12th and 71st New York State Militias paraded down the streets. Among those in the ranks was Private Francis Barlow of the 12th. Before the war was over, young Barlow would be a major general and have a knoll named for him at Gettysburg. In the 71st marched sons of prominent New York City physician, Dr. Samuel Ellis. Five Ellis brothers would participate in the upcoming battle in various commands.[16]

The next day, April 22nd, the 69th New York Militia was ready to leave.

> About three o'clock the order of march was given. The regiment moved into Broadway amid deafening cheers; flags and banners streamed from the windows and house-tops; ladies waved their handkerchiefs from balconies, and flung bouquets on the marching column. At the head of the procession was a decorated wagon, drawn by four horses, and bearing the inscription, "Sixty-ninth, remember Fontenoy," and "No North, no South, no East, no West, but the whole Union."[17]

Accompanying these Irishmen was a green banner, a flag honoring their homeland. The green background and harp reminded the men of their heritage. This regiment was destined to earn what is arguably the most famous reputation of any in the

---

[15] Henry G. Pearson, *James S. Wadsworth of Geneseo.* (New York: 1913), 61-63; William F. Fox, *New York at Gettysburg*, 3 Vols. (Albany, N.Y.: 1900), 1343-1344.

[16] *New York at Gettysburg*, 1353; *Honors of the Empire State in the War of the Rebellion*, 248. One of these men, Augustus Van Horne Ellis, would die while in command of another regiment at Gettysburg.

[17] Conyngham, *The Irish Brigade*, 21; Todd, *Seventy-Ninth Highlanders*, 2. "Fontenoy" refers to a battle where a brigade of Irishmen, who were fighting for the French, turned back a British breakthrough with a dramatic counterattack. Not only was this a brave act, but it was remembered because of its significance as a defeat over a British foe.

Colonel Elmer Ellsworth of the 11th New York Fire Zouaves

Miller's Photographic History of the Civil War

Union army, making famous charges and stands on numerous fields of battle throughout the war.[18]

Over the next week other commands marched from the city, but most citizens focused their attention on a new volunteer regiment forming, made up of city firemen. At the center of this effort was a New York native who achieved fame before the war touring with an elite zouave unit, amazing audiences with their marching and drill precision. His name was Elmer Ellsworth.

Ellsworth began organizing the "Fire Zouaves." This unit soon achieved notoriety not only for their famous commander and flashy uniforms – baggy red and blue outfits modeled after the French – but because of their conduct. This group of rowdy firemen would quickly prove themselves a handful in Washington.[19]

Through generous donations, Ellsworth's troops received uniforms and equipment, and on April 29th the 11th New York "Fire Zouaves" left the state. Within a brief time, the firemen were earning a reputation as roughnecks and rowdies in the Capital. When a fire broke out there in early May, Ellsworth's Zouaves crashed from their camp and rushed through the city streets to a firehouse. Finding the doors locked, they broke in and raced toward the scene with the commandeered fire engine. Within a few hours the blaze was extinguished. The grateful owner of Willard's Hotel, a neighboring structure saved by the efforts of the "Fire Zouaves," invited the New Yorkers to have a complimentary breakfast for their efforts. Although this act received much appreciation, it also reinforced their image as a wild lot.[20]

Within a few weeks tragedy struck the regiment. Colonel Ellsworth was given authority to march his men across the Potomac into Alexandria, Virginia – secession territory. While patrolling through the city, Ellsworth noticed a Confederate flag blatantly flying on a hotel rooftop. The colonel and some zouaves rushed into the building and to the top floor. After tearing the flag from the pole, they started down the stairs with their prize. Waiting for them was the owner of the establishment – carrying a loaded shotgun. The irate Southerner stepped into the stairwell and fired a fatal shot into Ellsworth's chest. The incident shocked the

---

[18] Conyngham, *The Irish Brigade*, 29.
[19] McKay, *The Civil War and New York City*, 71.
[20] Harrison Comings letter. *Voices of the Civil War: First Manassas*, 23.

country. This famous young leader, who inspired so many, was dead even before his men reached the battlefield.

While regiments from New York City were marching off to war, cities and villages in upstate New York were also mobilizing. War committees were established and meetings scheduled; soon companies and regiments were formed. Like New York City, these commands also included some interesting ethnic and professional groups. In Rochester, the first company formed were Germans, mostly immigrants who could speak little or no English, under Captain Adolf Nolte. Another company was primarily made up of firemen.[21]

Upstate units generally formed into new volunteer regiments, such as the 11th New York zouaves had, rather than existing militia commands. These regiments organized according to "General Orders No. 17," passed by the state on April 16, 1861. This order called for ten companies in each regiment, with each company composed of one captain, one lieutenant, one ensign, four sergeants, four corporals, two musicians, and sixty-four privates. New recruits would be accepted from ages 18 to 45, but minors with "the written consent of the parent, guardian or master" could be enlisted.[22]

The first two upstate units formed were the 12th, from Syracuse, Onondaga County, and the 13th, from Rochester, Monroe County. While these larger counties could support entire regiments, many smaller rural communities were busy raising companies. Upon signing on seventy-five-plus recruits, the company (or companies) would set off for a mustering point, usually Elmira, New York, where they would join other such commands to form a regiment.[23]

The following description, written by a new recruit during this period, gives a good feel of the scenes as the men left for the war.

---

[21] Rochester *Democrat and American*, April 25 and May 6, 1861.
[22] Copies of "General Orders No. 17" were printed in the newspapers. Rochester *Democrat and American*, April 27, 1861.
[23] The 12th New York was the "first rural regiment" – outside of New York City. "The Onondaga Regiment"

The village of Lyons was all astir at an early hour, and Military, Fire Companies, Associations, and Citizens generally, turned out in goodly numbers to escort, and bid God speed to the gallant band who had volunteered for the defense of the bulwarks of our free institutions – the Constitution and the Laws.[24]

This last statement, "the Constitution and the Laws," was very representative of why the men were fighting. This same theme was expressed in a slogan adopted by the 13th New York Volunteers: "God and our country is our motto." This gave meaning to why they were fighting, and one of the boys later stated, "We have strictly adhered to our motto."[25]

Fighting to sustain the Constitution and to preserve the Union were the primary motivational factors inspiring the men to enlist – combined with the adventure associated with the expected battle.

They gathered from the farm, from the workshop, from the factory; young men of fortune left luxurious homes for the camp and the field; native and foreign born alike came forward with common enthusiasm – all were seen rallying beneath a common flag, and exclaiming with one heart and voice, "The American Union, it must be and shall be preserved, cost what it may of treasure and of blood."[26]

The Spirit of '76 is gaining strength in our hearts. There is not a man among us I believe but had rather shed the last drop of his heart's blood than to survive and see

---

[24] "Wayne County in the Field" *Clyde Times Semiweekly*, May 8, 1861.

[25] Walter Fleming letter, June 4, 1861; Also A.G.C. letter, July 30, 1861.

[26] *Honors of the Empire State in the War of the Rebellion*, 21. It was only later in the war that the noble ideals of emancipation began inspiring larger numbers of troops. Slavery was such an abstract concept to most of these men that they openly stated they were not fighting to free the slaves, but to preserve the Union. In fact, abolitionists were viewed as extremists at this point. See R.L. Murray, *Before the Appointed Time*, (Wolcott, N.Y.: 2001), 16.

the stars and stripes trodden in the dust.... We hope of course, to see again our homes and those we love, but if not – if we shall be called to the battle-field to die – our last words shall be, "God and our native land!"[27]

Once the ranks of the companies and regiments were filled, the recruits began their brief training routine to prepare them for battle.

---

[27] R.D.L. letter, May 14, 1861.

Chapter Two

"Ill Feeling Among Our Patriotic Volunteers"

Once the companies were formed, one of the first functions they needed to perform was the election of officers and non-commissioned officers. Being a democratic society, it only made sense politically – but not necessarily militarily – for those leading the units to be elected. As previously stated, each company was composed of one captain, one lieutenant, one ensign, four sergeants, and four corporals – all of whom were elected.[1]

Once a sufficient number of companies were gathered, with their officers in place, the captains and lieutenants then selected their commanding officer, the colonel – and then a lieutenant colonel and a major.[2] In most cases this was merely a formality; a

---

[1] Soon afterwards, the regiments increased from a company size of seventy-five to one hundred (thus a regiment would be 1,000 men strong), and utilized two lieutenants instead of a lieutenant and an ensign. The number of sergeants and corporals were also increased proportionately. Electing non-commissioned officers, sergeants and corporals. "The Volunteer Regiment and 'General Orders Number One,' Issued by Gen. VanValkenburgh." Rochester *Democrat and American*, April 27, 1861; A.G.C. letter, May 10, 1861.

[2] "This is done under the law, by the several commissioned officers chosen by the companies…" "The Volunteer Regiment and 'General Orders Number One,' Issued by Gen. VanValkenburgh." Rochester *Democrat and American*, April 27, 1861.

prominent man had usually played an instrumental part in raising the regiment, with the understanding he would become the colonel. Fortunately, at this point in the war, many of these commanders had previous military experience, with several being West Point graduates.

Although many of the highest ranking officers had military experience, this was not the case for most captains or lieutenants. Thus, many units were indeed fortunate enough to have the services of either West Point cadets or veterans to help drill the men. The following is a description from a volunteer.

> Drilling, meanwhile, was vigorously prosecuted, and many will remember the old Mexican [War] soldier who acted as our drill master and whose sing-song 'Left! Left! Now you have it, d—n you, keep it, Left! Left!' amused us so much while under his manipulation.[3]

Many of the regiments formed in upstate New York went to Elmira for their training. The location was selected because of its combination of rail access, proximity to traveling south – being located in the Southern Tier – and the plains surrounding the town, which made ideal grounds for drilling the troops.[4]

Unfortunately, the town of Elmira was not prepared for the sudden influx of thousands of troops. They were only given days to prepare. Plans were quickly implemented to build barracks for housing the troops, but it would take time for these structures to be completed. In the mean time, the community opened their doors, literally, and men stayed almost anywhere a roof provided shelter. Accommodations varied from regiments staying in a barrel factory and hastily constructed shanties, to members of the 27th New York staying in the Baptist Church, where "each man has a pew to himself."[5]

While part of the 27th was staying in the church, conditions were actually very good. Aside from each man having his own pew, they were also well fed at a local restaurant.

---

[3] Todd, *Seventy-Ninth Highlanders*, 3.
[4] Article in *Lyons Republican*, May 24, 1861.
[5] "Knapsack" letter, May 7, 1861; Article in Rochester *Democrat and American*, May 16, 1861; C.E.E. letter , May 28, 1861.

We've adopted rather genteel and aristocratic habits since our arrival here – we have! We go to church every day, and board at the Delevan House. We breakfast at 8 o'clock in the morning, dine at 2 o'clock and take supper at 7 o'clock. We have very good grub, and no cause for complaint.[6]

The Delevan House treated the men so well the recruits purchased a silver pitcher and plate for the owners and employees.[7]

Before long, barracks were being completed. At first these were "temporary shelters hastily thrown up for the accommodation of the troops and partly of buildings already there," but soon "barracks consist[ing] of twenty shanties, about 90 feet by 18 feet" were ready and the regiments moved in. These buildings were located "one mile west of the business part of the village." Later in the war these barracks would be converted into a prisoner of war camp, housing Confederates.[8]

The arrival of thousands of troops created more problems for the residents of Elmira than just housing; suddenly, personal safety became an issue in this usually quiet city. A volunteer wrote home stating, "It is hardly safe for a man to travel the streets of Elmira after dark, unless he is fully armed." There were several murders committed during this period.[9]

Many of the first 5,000 troops arriving in Elmira brought with them two problems leading to potential violence and crimes. First, many of the new volunteers showed up in camp with knives and revolvers. The romantic perceptions of soldiers fighting it out in hand-to-hand combat prevailed, so men brought along personal weapons. In reality, however, these proved to be more dangerous to their own troops than to the enemy. The second problem was that when many of these recruits first arrived they were not offi-

---

[6] J.D.Mc. letter, May 14, 1861.

[7] C.E.E. letter, May 19, 1861; J.D.Mc. letter, May 14, 1861.

[8] J.C.G. letters, May 15 and June 28, 1861; C.E.E.. letter, May 28, 1861; Fairchild, *History of the 27th*, 5.

[9] J.D.Mc. letter, May 14, 1861; Fairchild, *History of the 27th*, 6.

cially mustered into units. Thus, they roamed about without officers to keep them in check.[10]

The following comment by a soldier in Elmira shows aspects of both of these problems. He wrote describing his comrades being called to put down a mutiny in a neighboring unit. Apparently, a group of men used to freely roaming about were put under a commander who tried to instill some discipline, and they rebelled.

We loaded our revolvers and buckled on our bowie-knives, as we fully expected there would be a fight. But the affair was nipped in the bud by the arrest of the ring-leader..."[11]

An officer from the Federal government was in Elmira to officially muster the troops unto United States service. The first regiments, such as the 12th and 13th New York Volunteers, signed on for a period of ninety days service to the Federal government, but as previously stated, they had already mustered into state service for two years (being assured that this would constitute duty inside the Empire State).[12] Within a few weeks, however, the situation had changed. Both the lawmakers in Albany and Washington saw the need for extending the length of service for the troops; this was no longer going to be merely a ninety days war. Thus, new units forming, such as the 27th New York Volunteers, mustered in for their full two-year term in Federal service.[13]

Not all recruits were pleased with the news. In fact, many refused to sign anything committing them to longer Federal ser-

---

[10] Rochester *Democrat and American*, May 14, 1861; C.W.M. letter, May 9, 1861. Carrying personal weapons was an issue early in the war. Later recruits were discouraged from bringing such items to camp.

[11] J.D.Mc. letter, May 14, 1861.

[12] Ensign Gilbert letter, July 27, 1861; Cazeau, *Account of the Thirteenth New York*, 2; "B." letter, June 10, 1861; "The Onondaga Regiment" Syracuse *Daily Journal*, May 4, 1861.

[13] The 27th was sworn in for two years of service in the first few days of July. They "took oath of allegiance to the United States for the term of two years, dating to the time of the state enlistment." A.W.T. letter, July 4, 1861. Also Nevins, *The Improvised War*, 167; Rochester *Democrat and American*, April 27, 1861.

vice. Although the news of extended terms was not popular with the men, the vast majority not only consented to it, but applied pressure to those refusing to sign. Some were taken by force, having half their faces shaved and then were "tossed in a blanket." Others were placed one at a time in a ring of troops, where the soldiers "jeered and hissed him." Under this indignation, many of those initially resisting consented, agreeing to the extended term.[14]

These enlistment episodes were not the only conflicts between soldiers in camp. While training in Elmira, two New York regiments nearly came to blows. Apparently, a private from the 27th New York was drunk and on returning to camp got into trouble with a neighboring regiment, the 33rd New York Volunteers. Walking past the headquarters of the 33rd, the intoxicated soldier stumbled and startled an officer's horse. A lieutenant standing nearby grabbed the man and knocked him down. When the colonel verbally lashed the drunk and he was pushed down again, the man picked up a stone and threw it at the colonel. The private was then arrested and placed in the regiment's guardhouse, being "gagged, bound, and chained to the floor, causing his mouth to bleed." News of his treatment, in "somewhat exaggerated" terms, reached the 27th just after their officers had retired to their quarters in town. Someone went for the colonel while the indignant troops gathered outside the barracks, contemplating means of retrieving their errant recruit. Upon his arrival, Colonel Henry Slocum, the commander of the 27th, praised his troops for their loyalty, but assured them they would not be allowed to free their comrade. He would deal with the situation in the morning.

The next morning tensions increased when the private somehow managed to escape from the guardhouse and came running back to the 27th's barracks, closely pursued by his captors. Members of the 27th quickly formed a protective wall, halting the angry guards, who in turn went back for reinforcements. The confrontation escalated as men armed with rocks and revolvers assembled, but the officers reacted quickly and averted a major incident. The soldier remained with his regiment, but received punishment from his own officers.[15]

---

[14] A.D.A. "Punishing a Renegade" letter, May 24, 1861; S.A.M. letter, May 22, 1861.

[15] "An Episode" (Anonymous) letter, June 15, 1861.

This incident was not the only source of irritation for the men of the 27th. Once the troops moved from town out to the new barracks, they found their meals to be somewhat less desirable than those cooked at the Delevan House and other facilities in the city. The food, in fact, got to be so bad that in protest members of the regiment kicked over dining tables and made a major commotion. One soldier remembered that this "ripping up of tables and smashing of things in general had inaugurated an immediate reform."[16]

Another soldier voiced his complaints in a letter to his hometown newspaper.

> The members of this regiment held an indignation meeting on Friday night, and passed resolutions censuring the authorities for using us as they do. Here we are, (or at least most of us), without money, clothed in rags, and fed much worse than the prisoners in the [County] Jail, and yet we are told that we are to have uniforms and pay the first of the week; but *that* time never comes.[17]

This quote is insightful in that it addresses three of the major complaints the recruits had: delay in payment, poor quality uniforms (and/or a delay in getting any uniforms), and poorly cooked rations. These three items were the most common subjects of complaint, along with a fourth, poor quality firearms. In some cases, these issues severely affected the men's morale.

Soldiers entering the service during this period were paid eleven dollars per month. This sum was very low, even in those days, considering a common laborer could expect to earn at least one dollar per day.[18] Compounding the low pay was the delay in getting the soldiers their money. As with everything else, the government was not prepared for the logistics of paying an army this

---

[16] C.T.B. letter, June 3, 1861; Fairchild, *History of the 27th*, 4.

[17] "B." letter, June 10, 1861.

[18] "A Volunteer's Complaint" *Lyons Republican*, June 21, 1861. In reality, a laborer could expect to earn more than one dollar per day, possibly up to sixty dollars per month. See R.L. Murray, *Before the Appointed Time: The History of the 108th New York Volunteers at Antietam.* (Benedum Books: 2001), 11. Just after the battle of Bull Run, Congress increased a private's wage to thirteen dollars per month.

large. It took time to organize and implement an efficient payroll network. Supposedly helping to supplement the recruit's pay were the contributions of the relief committees that were established "to support the families who have, and who wish to volunteer..."[19] At least one volunteer wrote home expressing his disgust for not only the Federal government's delay in payments, but also another issue, the Union Defense Committee's lack of effort in providing funds for his wife and children.

> It is reported here that they [the Union Defense Committee] have stoped giving any more money to the familys of the voolenteers. If it is so I want you to Let me know for I would not stay...[20]

Uniforms were another item creating grumbling among the troops. For many units the delay in receiving their military outfits was the issue, but for most it was the lack of quality in the uniforms supplied by the state. The first commands, such as the 12th and 13th New York Volunteers in Elmira, received what were quickly referred to as "shoddy" uniforms.

> [The colonel of the 12th New York reported] The uniform furnished by the State is a complete humbug, and an imposition on our volunteers. It is composed of a material that comes to pieces after one week's wear. The tailors of the regiment are busy all the while keeping them together long enough to reach the other side of the Potomac...[21]

> [Another soldier wrote home saying] ...we stand no comparison with the Scotch Highlanders (or any other regiment in the city) as far as uniforms are concerned.

---

[19] "Rochester for the Union!" Rochester *Union and Advertiser*, April 17, 1861; Rochester *Democrat and American*, April 24 and 25, 1861.

[20] Terry A. Johnston, Jr., ed. *"Him on One Side and Me on the Other" The Civil War Letters of Alexander Campbell, 79th New York Infantry Regiment and James Campbell, 1st South Carolina Battalion.* (University of South Carolina: 1999), 16. This was in the volunteer's own phonetic spelling.

[21] Colonel E. L. Walrath letter to Mayor Andrews (of Syracuse).

They look as neat as can be, while our men are ragged, and some of them very dirty. They do not take pride in keeping their clothes nice, for they are actually ashamed of their whole rigging. It is a shame to the State of New York, to have us here looking as we do, and as long as we are in condition we are now, you will never hear of anything very smart of us…any one to look at us would think we were just out of the Penitentiary, or off the canal.[22]

[A visitor to the camp of the 13th New York stated,] No one can visit encampments here without being humiliated, if a New Yorker, by the shameful conduct of the Empire State.[23]

Adding to the men's woes was the fact that while they were promised top quality muskets when enlisting, many commands in fact being assured they would get rifled muskets, what they received instead were poor quality antiquated weapons.[24]

The guns… [we received are] cast off muskets twenty years old and fifty years behind the age, instead of the Enfield Rifle, or Rifle musket promised.[25]

Our muskets are of the old Springfield pattern, altered from the flint to percussion, and it is a question of doubt to the soldier when he fires his piece, whether he will be found standing in the ranks after the discharge.[26]

For some units, such as the 27th New York, they were without any uniforms or weapons at all during their first five weeks in ser-

---

[22] B. Gilbert letter.

[23] C.P.D. letter, July 13, 1861.

[24] Byles Jr. letter, May 27, 1861; Rochester *Democrat and American*, May 21 and 28, 1861.

[25] "Grumbler" letter, June 4, 1861. Rochester *Democrat and American*, June 7, 1861.

[26] Col. E. L. Walrath letter to Mayor Andrews (of Syracuse).

vice. In fact, the officers were given walking sticks to distribute to help drill the men.[27]

These factors are important because they strongly affected the morale of the soldiers. "The condition of [our regiment] is indeed miserably confused," wrote one recruit, "and is fast breeding discontent and ill feeling among our patriotic volunteers."[28] Some men were so upset about the problems they took it upon themselves to go public with their complaints, sending editorials to their hometown newspapers. These articles created ill feelings and embarrassment for the officers of the regiments involved.

Articles in Rochester newspapers from members of the 13th New York complaining about their improper treatment and inadequate supply created such a stir, that the unit's commander, Colonel Isaac Quinby, had to publicly respond. Colonel Quinby first wrote the editors, questioning their judgment in printing these letters. Then he pointed out that the government was not prepared to provide "for a large army so suddenly called into service, and the machinery did not work smoothly."[29] Helping restore confidence at home and quieting the grumblings in camp were letters from other soldiers stating that many of the complaints were exaggerations; they wondered exactly what these whining soldiers expected, luxury accommodations? After all, they were in the army.[30]

Aside from the morale problems created within the regiments, the poor supplies, uniforms and antiquated guns created extra work for officers such as Colonel Quinby. Rather than spending his time training the men, Isaac Quinby was forced to make repeated trips to Washington and Albany to lobby for better provi-

---

[27] Rochester *Democrat and American*, May 11, 1861; C.E.E. letter, June 28, 1861; A.W.T. letter, June 30, 1861.

[28] "Illinois" letter, June 10, 1861. Rochester *Democrat and American*, June 13, 1861.

[29] Col. Isaac Quinby letter, June 17, 1861. Rochester *Union and Advertiser*, June 19, 1861. The regimental quartermaster also wrote a letter to the papers, explaining, "The Quartermaster cannot issue what is not furnished to him." O.L. Terry letter, June 16, 1861. Rochester *Democrat and American*, June 19, 1861.

[30] Typical among these was the "Ensign" letter, dated June 15, 1861, and appearing in the Rochester *Union and Advertiser*, June 19, 1861.

sions and arms. This was both mentally and physically draining on the colonel. A man under his command wrote home stating, "I need not say the cares of this Regiment are wearing upon him."[31]

---

[31] "Ensign" letter. June 27, 1861; also Rochester *Democrat and American*, June 27, 1861.

Chapter Three

"Fast Going to Pieces"

On May 29, 1861, the 12th and 13th New York State Volunteers marched down the main street in Elmira amidst a cheering crowd of civilians and fellow soldiers, and beneath a banner that read, "Onward to Victory." Coupled with the pride these two regiments felt, and the admiration of the remaining units, were feelings of disappointment. Although these troops were finally marching off to war to serve their country, they were doing so in shoddy uniforms and carrying antiquated weapons.[1]

> The troops that have left here were supplied with…the miserable uniforms furnished by the Brooks Brothers, of which so much complaint has justly been made…. [They also have] very poor arms; they are the old style musket, and are stamped "Springfield, 1841." It is said that they will shoot one man and kick over two at each discharge.[2]

The two regiments boarded three trains, thirty-five cars, and began their thirty-plus hour trip to Washington. Generally, the attitudes of the men were good, especially as they received welcomes and ovations along the way.

> We were cheered and regaled by the people during our passage through the State of Pennsylvania. Wherever we stopped, the inhabitants supplied us with hot coffee, cake,

---

[1] Rochester *Democrat and American*, May 30, 1861; J.S. letter, June 24, 1861; C.E.E. letter, June 5, 1861; "H" letter, June 24, 1861.
[2] J.S. letter, June 24, 1861.

milk and eggs. Some of the Pennsylvania Dutchmen brought us sour krout and speck.[3]

One soldier apparently enjoyed the ride a little too much; he managed to smuggle some alcohol on board, got drunk, and then fell off the train. Although badly injured, he was picked up, put back on the train, and traveled the rest of the way with the regiment.[4]

As the New Yorkers approached Baltimore, where the bridges had since been repaired, apprehensions grew. They heard the stories of the 6th Massachusetts and wondered what awaited them. One recruit remembered the scene.

> From village to village, from hamlet to hamlet, the people cheered us and gave us their blessing on our journey, until we arrived at Baltimore. There the scene changed. *The sinister looks of the populace made us aware that we trod on a volcano*; but as we had our muskets loaded, we did not mind their gloomy visages, and with a firm step and a watchful eye, we defiled through the very street where the 6th Massachusetts Regiment was attacked.[5]

As both regiments disembarked from the trains, they did so with muskets loaded. One man recalled they were "armed to the teeth – muskets at half cock." Their commanders decided not to maintain a low profile in the face of these "traitors," but instead the regimental musicians were playing and regimental flags boldly waved. Marching at the head of the 13th was the "matron" of the regiment, Mrs. Lucinda Briscoll. A widow with two sons in the unit, she received permission to accompany the 13th, serving as cook and laundress for Colonel Quinby and some of the officers. She became known as the "Mother of the Regiment."[6]

The 12th and 13th New York Volunteers arrived in Washington well after midnight. They soon were provided quarters and

---

[3] John Lewis letter.

[4] Lucinda Briscoll letter, May 31, 1861.

[5] John Lewis letter.

[6] Walter letter, June 4, 1861; Lucinda Briscoll letter, May 31, 1861.

then tents, and quickly got back to training for battle. For most of these upstate men, this was their first time in Washington. Although most were impressed with the sights, others were not.

> My idea of Washington and its glorious Palaces, has evaporated. It looks to me more like Palmyra's ruins, with its desolation, than the Capital of a great nation.[7]

Before long, the regiments were ordered across the Potomac into Virginia. This was both exciting and a refreshing change from the crowded and much used camps in the city.

> We enjoy life immensely now. The nearer we come to the enemy the better the men are pleased. Our camp is on high ground, and no danger from fever or ague, as there was in our last encampment.[8]

The "fever" and other sickness associated with the camps were the largest killers of the Civil War. Many more men died from disease than bullets. In the 13th New York, for example, they had already buried one recruit in Elmira and now another died, this one from measles, once they reached Washington. Aside from changing camp, another precaution was taken to prevent further deaths. "The whole regiment was vaccinated this morning," wrote a soldier, "to be on guard against the small pox."[9]

For those who were healthy, however, this period was an exciting time. One soldier wrote home saying they were in "full anticipation of an attack every night." Another explained they expected an attack from thousands of Confederates at any time.[10] These apprehensions made for some interesting evenings in camp.

---

[7] John Lewis letter.

[8] Ensign" letter. June 22, 1861.

[9] Rochester *Democrat and American*, June 22nd and 26th, issues, 1861; "Ensign" letter. June 15, 1861.

[10] S.A.M. letter, June 7, 1861. But he later stated that once night after night had passed, "we are beginning to fancy that the chances of it coming are less and less." Also, Walter Fleming letter, June 4, 1861.

Fall in! Fall in! We are attacked. Every man was up in an instant and seized the first articles of clothing that came to hand, putting them on, haphazard, in the dark, and grasping their muskets, rushed out to the parade ground. Some appeared with nothing on but their pants…[11]

This particular "attack" turned out to be two intoxicated soldiers trying to sneak back into camp. The most notorious unit for rushing out for these false alarms appears to have been the 69th New York, the Irishmen. A witness recalled:

…the 69th were always on the *qui vice* for an attack. If a cow bellowed at night, out would rush the 69th, double quick step towards Ball's Cross Roads, sure it was the guns of the enemy. Back they would return quite crest fallen. The camp would be quiet. A dog would bark in the direction of Fairfax – away, pell mell, up the hill would come the whole regiment, sure it was a secession cannon.[12]

The danger associated with an eminent attack inspired many soldiers to do some soul searching. One young man, a recent college graduate that enlisted in the 13th New York, took the time to write a serious letter to his father. His writing reveals not only their expectancy of being attacked, but also his devotion to duty.

Dear Father,
I have just received yours [letter], and have only time to send you a few lines. True, we have been ordered to take our position on the extreme right of McDowell's column encamped here [position of honor], and have received orders to hold it in case of a night attack, until morning, at all hazards. We shall fight soon. As I wrote you before, I wish to be buried in Lima if I fall, and it is possible. If not, remember me. I shall never flinch on the field. Do not fear for that. You shall never blush for any

---

[11] Todd, *Seventy-Ninth Highlanders*, 11.
[12] "Carrie" letter, June 29, 1861.

thing I shall do on the battle field. My hold on life is as dear to me as anybody's, but I would rather die than live dishonest, or see the flag above me struck to traitors.[13]

Unfortunately, not all the men were as dedicated to the cause as the young man above. Some soldiers refused to adapt to military life. Those causing the worst problems were court marshaled and drummed out of the service. In the 13th New York, one man was paraded out of the regiment after he threatened to shoot an officer. Here is how a member of the regiment described the scene.

J. Eastman has been drummed out of service. The drum corps and three men conducted him out of camp, the music being "The Rogues March." Eastman stood erect in the position of a soldier, and kept step with the music. The guard accompanied him to Georgetown. This is the end of him as far as we are concerned.[14]

Another man in the 13th was punished – marching eight miles a day for twelve successive days in full pack of sixty pounds – in response to an episode with Colonel Quinby. The colonel had previously issued an order forbidding side arms being carried by soldiers in the ranks – there were too many accidental shootings. One day, Quinby saw a soldier with a gun and demanded it be turned over to his captain. The man refused, declaring this order violated the Second Amendment, his right to bear arms. He was arrested and his gun confiscated.[15]

---

[13] T. L. Bowman letter to his father.

[14] "Ensign" letter. June 22, 1861.

[15] *Ibid.,* and article in Rochester *Democrat and American,* June 26th and 27th issues, 1861; Two men were accidentally shot when a member of the 13th N.Y.'s musket went off as they passed down Pennsylvania Avenue. A.O.C. letter, June 3, 1861; Also, a member of 13th was shot through the legs in camp. Walter Fleming letter, June 4, 1861; also Rochester *Union and Advertiser,* July 18, 1861; A soldier in the 14th Brooklyn was accidentally shot and killed while cleaning his gun in camp. C.V. Trevis, *The History of the Fighting Fourteenth* (New York: 1911), 216.

Colonel Quinby was not the only commander having troubles with his men. In several units, especially the 12th, the 13th and other upstate regiments that had been poorly equipped, there was much complaining and dissatisfaction. Further affecting the attitudes were rumors the men would have their ninety-day enlistments extended for two years. Colonel Walrath of the 12th wrote the mayor of Syracuse explaining the situation.

We were mustered into the service for three months, and it was expected at the time that we would be willing to remain longer. But this failure on the part of the State to give good uniforms to the men, has caused great dissatisfaction throughout the regiment, and it will be hard work to keep them in service longer than the time they were mustered into service.[16]

Soldiers made the following comments.

There is a strong determination among the men to leave the service at the expiration of three months. This is safe – nothing can save it. There is great dissatisfaction among the men, but I propose to let each one give his own experience.[17]

I think the men are determined to stay only three months. They speak indignantly of the State of New York. She has been no provident to them.[18]

The probability is, that very few of the men will go for any longer time [than ninety days], unless in some other regiment.[19]

There is some talk of our regiment being held here for the two years we were sworn in to the State service, and

---

[16] Col. E. L. Walrath letter to Mayor Andrews.
[17] "Friend C." letter, June 24, 1861.
[18] C.P.D. letter, July 7, 1861.
[19] A.G.C. letter, July 7, 1861.

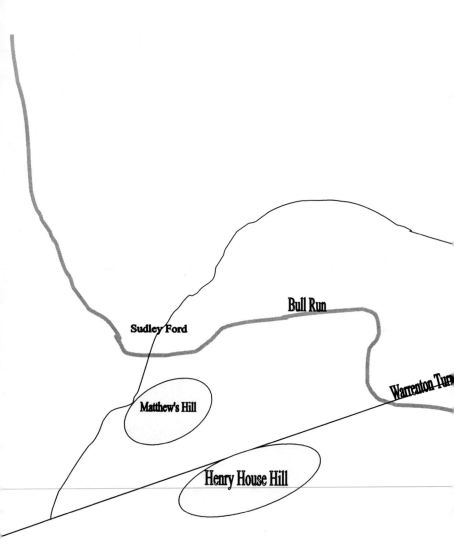

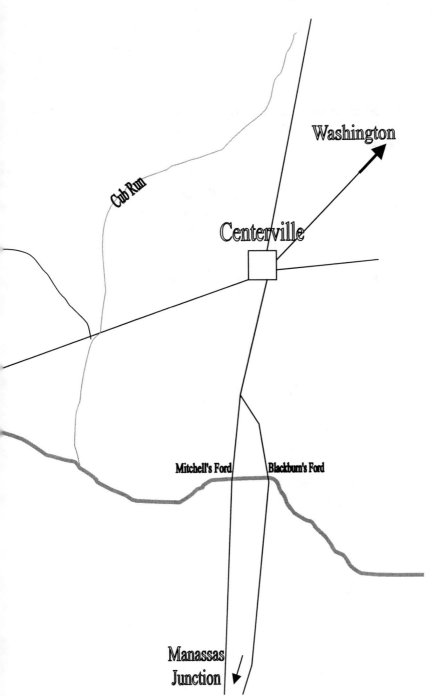

then again there are rumors of our being sent home in a few days.[20]

The above excerpt shows an ironic new development for the 13th New York. Along with the rumor of extended service, another buzz was circulating, that the regiment was instead going to be disbanded and sent home. These stories greatly intensified after Congressman Alfred Ely, representing the 13th New York's district, visited camp.[21]

The principle conversation around camp is about being disbanded. A thousand and one stories are afloat today. The burden of the song is that Col. Quinby has resigned, and his resignation has been accepted, and that we shall be sent home the 2nd of July. The regiment, I think, almost to a man, will refuse to swear in the U.S. service longer than three months, and if the citizens [back home] could be in our places three days, there would not be word of censure passed upon our return. We know that the government is both able and willing to supply us better, and therefore we complain.[22]

Additionally, another thing irritating the upstate men was the supposed better treatment that most of the New York City regiments received. This was even addressed by the politicians and newspapers back home. The theme of their contention was that because many downstate units, called "pet regiments" or "pet lambs," had "influential and wealthy friends, and what is better still, friends in court [the Legislature and Congress]," they received better treatment, uniforms, supplies and equipment. It was difficult enough for the men to endure shoddy uniforms and poor

---

[20] William Fleming letter, June 26, 1861.

[21] A.G.C. letter, July 7, 1861.

[22] "Friend E." letter, June 23, 1861. He added an interesting analogy comparing their conditions to those of the troops during the American Revolution. Those troops suffered because the government had nothing to give them. These troops currently in Washington were angry because their current government could supply them better – they felt – but refused to do so. Also "Haversack" letter, July 9, 1861.

weapons, but believing that others received better because of influential connections increased their dissatisfaction.

Fortunately, amidst all the problems facing the men of the 13th, some factors worked to increase their morale. First, rumors circulated that new rifles were on the way. In fact, through tireless lobbying and trips to Albany, Colonel Quinby managed to procure rifles for his troops. The colonel brought a sample back to camp, which increased the men's resolve, as the following letter excerpts show.[23]

> [The new weapons] are the Remington rifle, with the sword bayonet – a very nice, graceful and well made arm; they are looked for with much anxiety by the whole regiment, and will tend much to allay the constant grumbling. The boys feel much safer with them, as they will not "kill them at the breech" [reference to fear of their antiquated guns exploding when discharged].[24]

> We are in daily expectation of receiving our rifles, and these once obtained, we only ask one thing more, and that is the order to "Forward March." As it is, we keep our knapsacks packed, in hourly expectation of moving forward…[25]

The expectation of marching orders also increased morale. The excitement of a pending battle, and the opportunity to put an end to their service experience through a dramatic victory, helped encourage the men. An additional influence was the arrival of new uniforms.

In the third week of June, the 13th New York received new clothes. Finally, they hoped to replace their shoddy gray "Brooks Brothers" outfits, which were falling apart, with fine ones worn by

---

[23] Colonel Quinby returned from Albany with a "sample Remington rifle." "A Private's letter."

[24] A.G.C. letter, July 7, 1861.

[25] R. J. letter, June 22, 1861.

most of the other units. Coats and pants of "U.S. regulation" were distributed, "linen pants and blue sack coats."[26]

Unfortunately, the inferiority of these uniforms was soon apparent. First, a majority of the pants and coats were too small. Also, the pants turned out to be different colors – some blue and some brown. There were also not enough to go around, and once all the outfits were distributed, they were "fast going to pieces" – another batch of shoddy clothes.[27] With this new development, the outcry was so loud that the Attorney General of New York personally traveled to Washington and visited their camp. After inspecting the uniforms, he vowed that new ones, provided by New York, would be there as soon as possible.[28]

---

[26] "Ensign" letter. June 15, 1861; A.G.C. letter, June 17, 1861; R. J. letter, June 22, 1861.

[27] Article in Rochester *Democrat and American*, June 22, 1861; "Friend C." letter, June 24, 1861; R. J. letter, June 22, 1861; Sam Partridge letter, July 24, 1861. Blake McKelvey, ed. *Rochester in the Civil War.* (Rochester, N.Y.: 1944), 83.

[28] Capt. Schoeffel letter, July 7, 1861.

Chapter Four

"On to Richmond!"

> [New] regiments are crossing [the Potomac into Virginia] every hour of the day and night – their tramp, the rattle of the drums, the rumbling of their trains of baggage wagons, and the shouts of drivers, are continually heard...[1]

As the month of July 1861 progressed, thousands more Union troops arrived in Washington. Many were from New York, both traveling from New York City and the rendezvous in Elmira. Among these was the 27th New York, the "Union Regiment." This command consisted mainly of companies formed near Rochester and Binghamton. An observer noted, "The 27th is well uniformed and equipped, and contrasts strongly with some of the 'shoddy' regiments from our State."[2]

While these new units were streaming into Washington, the commander of the field army, Brigadier General Irwin McDowell, was trying to figure out how best to use them in battle. Given the opportunity, he would have preferred remaining in camp to better train the men. Then, gradually, undertake limited maneuvers to give the troops some experience marching and fighting in the field. Unfortunately, political pressure demanded that he lead his army out to face the Southern forces. The Northern population was tired of Rebel troops in such close proximity to the Capital. They were also disappointed by news concerning the first engagement

---

[1] "Haversack" letter, July 9, 1861.
[2] C.P.D. letter, July 13, 1861.

of the war, a small skirmish known as Big Bethel near Fort Monroe in eastern Virginia, which resulted in a Confederate victory.[3]

Leading the cries of "On to Richmond!" were the newspaper editors in New York City. These papers greatly influenced public opinion, and they made the process seem all too simple. Merely take the army south and defeat the Confederates; then drive on to Richmond, thus ending the rebellion. Naturally, the newspapermen had no idea how difficult it would be to lead these civilian soldiers on the march and then into battle. An officer in McDowell's army even made a public appeal for the "On to Richmond!" demands to cease. In an editorial he cautioned against pushing the army out into the field before it was ready, but this did little to dampen the demands being made.[4]

Aside from this pressure, General McDowell also had another reality to face – many of his ninety-day troops' enlistments would soon expire, and there were no guarantees, as the letter excerpts above clearly stated, that the soldiers would re-enlist. He needed to use the army he had, and he needed to use it soon.[5]

Although Irwin McDowell had never commanded an army before, he did manage to formulate a fairly impressive plan. The main effort would be a southward thrust with his army of roughly 30,000 men, to face a smaller force commanded by Brigadier General Pierre Gustave Toutant Beauregard – probably near Centerville or Manassas Junction. Hoping to use his superior numbers in a flanking movement, he would force his opponent back toward Richmond. McDowell wanted to avoid a pitched bat-tle, if possible, until they closed on the capital.[6]

Major General Robert Patterson, an aging and ineffective Union commander, would be a key to McDowell's success or fail-ure in this action. Patterson commanded a force of approximately 18,000 men at Harper's Ferry, Virginia. The presence of this force threatened the Shenandoah Valley. Thus a sizeable army of Con-

---

[3] William C. Davis, *Battle at Bull Run: A History of the First Major Campaign of the Civil War.* (Stackpole Books reprint: original 1977), 72.

[4] "An Officer of the Army" letter. *New York Times.*

[5] Also see Davis, *Battle at Bull Run*, 87. The 7th New York Militia had long since returned to New York when their enlistment term expired.

[6] Davis, *Battle at Bull Run*, 74; Davis, *First Blood*, 111.

Brigadier General Irwin McDowell
Commander of the Union forces at First Bull Run

Miller's Photographic History of the Civil War

federates was deployed to block their advance. All McDowell asked of Patterson was to make demonstrations, threatening an advance, to keep the 12,000 Confederate troops there occupied. If this force, commanded by Brigadier General Joseph E. Johnston, moved east and combined with Beauregard's army, McDowell would be in trouble. Unfortunately for the Federals, Patterson was ineffective and Johnston's army not only moved east in time to participate in the upcoming battle, but played a major role in the Confederate victory.

Rumors of impending marching orders circulated throughout the camps in Washington. Many regimental commanders took this opportunity to make last minute preparations. Colonel Walrath, of the 12th New York Volunteers, wrote home saying, "We expect soon to have an opportunity to trying the mettle of the boys." But before the trial, he wanted more practice. He took his men on a maneuver in some woods to see how they performed off the parade grounds. Before many days, his men would see action in just such terrain.[7]

With the army about to move, many important political officials made their way to camp, wishing their acquaintances and hometown units well. Among those visiting was Secretary of State Seward, of Auburn, New York. Along with greetings, the Secretary brought encouraging news. General George McClellan had just fought and won a small battle in western Virginia. Seward asked the officers to spread the word to their men.[8]

Orders were issued; be ready to move at a moment's notice. The increased activity convinced the men that this was for real. Many wrote final letters to family and friends, then left them with visitors from home – just in case something happened in combat. One visitor remembered the scene as men came to her with letters for loved ones and requests to be sent home for burial if they fell. She recalled an especially touching moment when a man stepped forward to give her a letter and a recent picture of himself in uniform.

---

[7] Col. E. L. Walrath letter, July 12, 1861.
[8] *Ibid.*

[He] left us a picture for his wife, and, said he, that is all the picture she will ever have of me, and this, showing us the picture of his wife and children, is all I have left me now. I shall have this buried with me if I die.[9]

On July 15th, official marching orders were received; they would move out the next day. The following is a description of events in the 69th New York's camp that evening.

The enthusiastic night was, accordingly, spent in various avocations by officers and men. Many went to confession, nearly all wrote home to their friends the exciting news, sending large sums of money which had been just received, while many others gave loose rein to fun and jollification, as numberless empty bottles and kegs could amply testify. Very little sleep was enjoyed by any one.[10]

On July 16, the march opening the Bull Run Campaign commenced. For most, it was a time of excitement – they would be participating in what many called "The greatest battle of the age."[11] No longer would they have to sit idly by and hear the old veterans of the War of 1812 and the Mexican War recount their glorious exploits; now they would have stories of their own to tell.

Surprisingly, not everyone believed the upcoming battle would be that big a deal. One veteran recalled:

We did not believe the enemy would seriously retard our progress, and the campaign was looked upon more in the nature of a pleasant excursion, with just that amount of danger which served to make it more interesting, than a military advance against an enemy.[12]

Veterans of later battles, during the course of the next three years, would remember how different this excursion was than future marches. An officer in the 14th Brooklyn remembered the

---

[9] "Carrie" letter, July 18, 1861.
[10] Conyngham, *The Irish Brigade*, 26.
[11] J.D.M. letter.
[12] Todd, *Seventy-Ninth Highlanders*, 21.

enthusiasm and naiveté present in this march that were lacking in later actions. He noted how the upcoming experience would change them.

> ...[Before his first battle the soldier] is enthusiastic and sees only the glory of combat. But on seeing the gloomy and awful scenes that result from battle, be it a victory or defeat... he is not so anxious for a second fight, and goes into it rather more reluctantly than enthusiastically.[13]

Another difference was their appearance. Aside from the occasional gray uniforms mixed into the Federal ranks, including some worn by the 13th New York, the soldiers also wore Havelocks on their heads. Havelocks were pieces of white cloth hanging out from the back of the cap, to shield the men's necks from the sun. They were modeled after the British troops in India and Crimea, and the French in Solferino. British officers supposedly supplied the pattern for the cap cover to ladies in Washington and New York City, and women all over made them for the troops. One veteran recalled, "The only good purpose they served, however, was to furnish lint and bandages for the wounded, and were never much worn after this battle."[14]

The men marched light. Cumbersome knapsacks and heavy baggage were left in camp. Most carried only their muskets and ammunition, a canteen and haversack with three days rations, and a blanket rolled up and placed diagonally over a shoulder.[15] Even with this, the march was slow, especially compared to later standards. The men were lax and allowed their lines to spread too far and were constantly wandering off to fill their canteens and hunt blackberries. Also showing the amateur status of the troops was

---

[13] *History of the Fighting Fourteenth*, 227.
[14] "Havelocks" article, Rochester *Democrat and American*, May 14, 1861, but originally printed in the New York *Times*, May 6, 1861; Fairchild, *History of the 27th*, 15.
[15] M.R.W. letter, July 18, 1866; Fairchild, *History of the 27th*, 9; A.W.T. letter, July 18, 1861; Davis, *Battle at Bull Run*, 93; A.B.M. letter, July 24, 1861; J.D.M. letter.

Drawing of a Union soldier in uniform,
with a Havelock attached to his cap.

Drawing from *Battles and Leaders of the Civil War.*

the fact that at least three men were accidentally shot on the march.[16]

Near the end of the first day's march, as most of the troops approached Fairfax Court House, they expected their first clash. They were disappointed to learn, however, that the Confederates had previously retired, leaving the small town unoccupied. "The Court House is by far the best building in the place," recalled a rural New York soldier taking in the sights, "but it is much inferior to many of the horse barns [back home.]"[17]

Bugles sounded in the early morning hours of July 17, and the army was soon stirring, preparing for the day's march. Once on the road, the men proceeded "slowly, very slowly."[18]

McDowell's army was divided into five divisions, but only his first three marched toward Bull Run and became engaged in battle on July 21st. Brigadier General Daniel Tyler commanded the First Division, containing fifteen regiments, including the 2nd, 69th and 79th New York State Militia units, and the 12th and 13th New York Volunteers. Colonel David Hunter commanded the Second Division, sixteen regiments, including the 8th, 14th, and 71st New York State Militia commands, and the 27th New York Volunteers. Colonel Samuel P. Heintzelman's Third Division, included eleven regiments, with two New York units, the 11th (Fire Zouaves) and the 38th Volunteers.[19]

Each division constituted a column of McDowell's advance. Taking different routes, they planned to converge on Centerville. Brigadier General Daniel Tyler's column took the northernmost route, and on the 17th approached Germantown. Felled trees slowed their progress, along with other obstacles left by the Confederates. Additionally, straggling was an increasing problem.

---

[16] Davis, *Battle at Bull Run*, 94; Captain John Breslin of the 69th was severely wounded when a musket carried by one of his soldiers fell from the stack in camp and discharged. Conyngham, *The Irish Brigade*, 29; Joseph G. Bilby, *Remember Fontenoy! The 69th New York and the Irish Brigade in the Civil War*. (Hightstown, N.J.:1995), 11.

[17] H.H.W. letter, July 19, 1861; C.W.M. letter, July 24, 1861.

[18] M.R.W. letter, July 18, 1861.

[19] *War of the Rebellion: Official Records of the Union and Confederate Armies.* Series I, 128 Vols. (Washington: 1880), Vol. 2, 314-315. Cited hereinafter as *O.R.*, Vol. 2.

Colonel William T. Sherman,
in command of a brigade at First Bull Run.
Pictured here as a major general later in the war.

Miller's Photographic History of the Civil War

Uniforms of the 79th New York "Highlanders"

Drawing from *Battles and Leaders of the Civil War*

One of Tyler's brigades was commanded by Colonel William T. Sherman, who would later lead armies in the West under Grant and march his columns through Georgia late in the war. Three of Sherman's four regiments were New Yorkers, the 69th and 79th Militia units and the 13th Volunteers. The fourth was the 2nd Wisconsin. Along the march Sherman's men were leisurely dropping out of ranks to do some foraging. The colonel responded by issuing orders against disturbing private property.[20]

Officers rode up and down the line warning the men to leave the local farmers' animals alone. These undisciplined raw soldiers were little impressed by these messengers and often yelled back at them, going about their business as they pleased. About this time an episode occurred in the ranks of the 79th New York "Highlanders." The 79th New York was formed in New York City and made up mainly of Scots. Modeling their militia unit after a famous Scottish command, the "Highlanders," their dress uniform was a kilt with traditional Scottish accessories. While in the field, however, the kilts were set aside and a fatigue uniform of "blue jackets and Cameron tartan trousers" was to be worn. In reality, most of the men during this campaign were wearing the regulation blue uniforms.[21]

A member of the regiment remembered an interesting incident as the 79th passed a small farm.

> Captain -------- had insisted on wearing the kilts when we started on the march. "The Highlanders," he said, "wear the kilts in India, and surely the gnats and mosquitoes of Virginia are not so troublesome as the venomous insects of the East." Being the only member thus arrayed he was a conspicuous figure. His love for fresh pork, and utter disregard of orders, led him, with drawn sword, to give chase to a young pig. The chase was an exciting one; as the captain ran, his kilts flew up, and his long, gaunt legs were exposed.... [When] the pig squeezed under the lowest rail [of a fence] the captain threw himself over the top one, and in the act made such an exhibition of his

---

[20] Davis, *Battle at Bull Run*, 96.
[21] Todd, *Seventy-Ninth Highlanders*, 1 and 18.

anatomy as to call forth a roar of laughter from all who witnessed it...[22]

This was not the only foraging story the 79th was involved with. While passing through Germantown, members of the Highlanders found some beehives.

[T]he air was soon 'blue' with bees, curses and imprecations; man ran hither and thither trying to shake off their tormentors, while mounted officers put spurs to their horses and beat a hasty retreat.[23]

Members of the 79th were not the only ones looking for food on the march, as the following letter excerpts demonstrate.

Our march to Germantown was interrupted by numerous trees, that the rebels had used to blockade the road. Two houses were burned to the ground [most likely set by retiring Confederate troops], and numerous trophies found; hogs, sheep, chickens, &c., were captured, cooked, and devoured in short order.[24]

...I must confess that the boys committed some very unjustifiable depredations. Poultry, pigs, butter, cheese, everything eatable was, as we say, "snatched" and appropriated.[25]

[On the march]...there was considerable butchering done among the unfortunate animals: several pigs, large number of chickens, turkeys, &c., and one large bull met an unwept death. Some one found a bee-hive which they brought into camp. It was fun and no mistake, when they broke it open, to see the boys dance the break-down as the bees got out. You may be sure there was some tall

---

[22] *Ibid.*, 21.

[23] *Ibid.*, 19.

[24] A.G.C. letter, July 20, 1861.

[25] A.T.W. letter, July 18, 1861.

kicking and rubbing among the boys when those little "hot-footed" fellows got at them.[26]

When the Union troops went into camp on the evening of July 17, the only "hostiles" they had encountered had been those bees and some irate farmers. This would not be the case the next day, however, as General Tyler moved his troops into Centerville, then pushed beyond town toward Bull Run Creek. Here he would exceed his authority and bring on an engagement at Blackburn's Ford – which directly involved the 12th New York Volunteers from Onondaga County.

---

[26] J.D.M. letter.

Chapter Five

"Give Us Rifles, and

We Will Rally"

On July 17, 1861, Brigadier General Daniel Tyler's division was camped just outside of Centerville. General McDowell instructed Tyler to push his troops on into the village the next day, and then move south, toward Mitchell's and Blackburn's Fords. McDowell hoped Tyler's effort of threatening a general assault from these fords would hold the Confederate's attention, while another column moved on Beauregard. McDowell sent General Heintzelman's column to turn the enemy's right flank. As Heintzelman moved, McDowell gave Tyler some final instructions, "Do *not* bring on an engagement."[1]

While Tyler's troops camped just outside of Centerville on the 17th, a citizen rode through the lines of the 12th New York. Unexpectedly, the man turned in his saddle, yelled, and fired a few shots. Not long after this another rider approached the sentries and was stopped. Producing a letter from Secretary of War Cameron giving him permission to go where he pleased, the rider expected immediate passage. Colonel Walrath of the 12th, however, decided not to honor the letter. The rider bellowed, "Do you know who I am, sir? I am Henry J. Raymond of the New York *Tribune*." Walrath replied that since the previous incident he was under orders not to allow *anyone* to pass. Raymond became indignant and tried

---

[1] William C. Davis and the editors of Time-Life. *First Blood: Fort Sumter to Bull Run.* (Time-Life Books: 1983), 117.

to force his way through the post. Walrath temporarily placed him under arrest.

This small incident would have some serious repercussions for the 12th New York. In the days following the upcoming battle, this same Henry Raymond would write a widely distributed account of the conflict. Not surprisingly, his depiction was uncomplimentary to both Colonel Walrath and the 12th – he called their conduct at Blackburn's Ford "cowardly." In fact, this article was so damaging, Walrath later requested a court of inquiry to examine the charges.[2]

Early on July 18, Tyler's division, with Colonel Israel Richardson's brigade in the lead, passed through Centerville. The column turned south, on the road heading directly for Manassas Junction, and began their march toward Bull Run Creek. General Tyler and Colonel Richardson rode ahead of their troops for a closer look at the enemy positions. On reaching an elevation, they could see the ford, guarded, apparently, only by a few Confederate pickets. Across the stream an enemy battery was also visible. Tyler suspected there were more troops in the area, so he decided to advance his force.

Richardson's brigade was ordered up, along with two 20-pounder artillery pieces. Skirmishers went forward while the cannon unlimbered and prepared for action. Gunfire erupted as the Federals advanced. Ignoring orders not to bring on an engagement, and the warnings of one of McDowell's staff officers on the scene, Tyler instead increased his effort. More artillery and infantry deployed; he sent three regiments off to the right and ordered the 12th New York into line on the battery's left. Soon more artillery pushed forward, to an even more exposed position.[3]

Commanding the cannon rumbling toward Bull Run Creek was Captain Romeyn Ayres. A Herkimer County, New York, na-

---

[2] "Leaves From an Officer's Diary – The 12th New York Regiment of Volunteers at Blackburn's Ford." Syracuse *Courier and Union*, November 11, 1880. "Cowardly" newspaper comments see E. P. Woodford letter; Col. E. L. Walrath letter, July 28, 1861. In Raymond's article Colonel Walrath was said to have abandoned the regiment, supposedly seen "galloping across the field to a safe retreat." Both Walrath and his regiment were exonerated by the Court of Inquiry.

[3] Davis, *First Blood*, 118.

tive, he had graduated from West Point in 1847. In the following years he would rise to be chief of artillery at the division and corps level, and then commanded an infantry brigade with the rank of brigadier general.[4]

Ayres' two artillery pieces quickly drew fire from the enemy. As soon as he deployed, the Confederate line erupted and the captain's command was in trouble – his guns were isolated and all the horses on one limber were shot down.[5]

Meanwhile, the 12th New York was still deploying. An officer in the Onondaga County regiment remembered the events.

> We arrived at a position to the left of a heavy wood, where we were covered in part by a thick undergrowth of light brush and then halted. An artillery officer came out of the wood and ordered us into it to support his battery, which he said was being cut up. The colonel [Walrath] saw Col. Richardson (the commander of our brigade) down toward the left and asked him if we should go. *After hesitating*, he said, "Yes, go in and drive them out," and never were men more eager for the fray than were ours.[6]

Colonel Walrath ordered his men to remove their blankets and "all superfluous clothing" before entering the woods. Although, as the officer stated above, they were "eager for the fray," Colonel Walrath also recognized some apprehensions.

> Our Regiment had the old muskets and were in miserable condition; about three in five were in condition for firing. Our cartridges were of different sizes. Some would almost drop in the barrel, while others would require the utmost exertion to get the ball home. The men had no confidence in their pieces, which was one of the reasons

---

[4] Fox, *New York at Gettysburg*, 1361.

[5] *O.R..*, Vol. 2, 311 and 313; Davis, *Battle at Bull Run*, 117. Ayres sent a lieutenant forward with a limber to retrieve the gun. By then the Confederate fire had dwindled and the men hitched the piece and headed safely for the rear.

[6] Ira Wood letter, July 23, 1861.

why they [had problems standing and fighting later in the engagement].[7]

As the 12th entered their first combat, they had more than just poor weapons working against them. The terrain was rough and uneven, making it difficult to advance while maintaining proper alignment and communication. Additionally, the 12th New York numbered at this time between 700 to 800 men. As the war progressed, regiments were usually half this size when entering the battlefield – due to previous combat losses and disease. Thus, conducting this long line of raw recruits into battle would be difficult.[8]

[The regiment] formed in good order and marched boldly forward, each officer viewing with the other their whole duty to themselves and their country. – The ground was uneven, being filled with deep ravines, hilly slopes, and deep gulley [sic], which retarded the progress of our troops, yet they bore steadily on until they reached the edge of the wood, when it was apparent from the nature of the ground, that the left wing of the regiment must of necessity be in advance of the right, towards the enemy's battery...[9]

We marched right up on to the edge of the ravine that separated us and the enemy. And our left wing rested in front of a masked battery. We could not cross the ravine on account of its great depth, nor could we see a single man to shoot at, so perfectly had they screened themselves.[10]

The brush was so thick that we could not keep any kind of line. The advance was more of a charge than an advance, and no one knew where or how far the enemy were from us, or what their position was. In that condi-

---

[7] Colonel E. L. Walrath letter, July 28, 1861.
[8] The 12th New York Volunteers number just over 800 men at enlistment. "The Onondaga Regiment" Syracuse *Daily Journal*, May 4, 1861.
[9] E.C.B. letter, July 30, 1861.
[10] E. P. Woodford letter.

tion the right had to descend a bank, the center to leap a fence, and the left going down a side hill.[11]

From these descriptions of the initial stage of the advance, we see just how challenging it was for the men. Keeping the different wings of the regiment advancing as a cohesive group would be difficult, especially when the Confederates opened fire.

After crossing the fence and starting down the hill, the regiment suddenly received a dramatic volley of musketry. Fortunately, the Confederates were aiming too high, for as one member of the 12th said, had the enemy fire "been well directed, [it] would have swept every man into eternity."[12]

Officers shouted, "Down! Lie down, men!" The men dropped to the ground and prepared to return fire.[13]

> The only way we could direct our fire was by aiming at the spot where we saw the flash of their guns. We at once charged upon them and then fell flat upon the ground, and loaded again. Before we arose their second volley was fired which came lower and did us more injury than the first. If we had not fallen upon the ground I am sure we could not have escaped the destruction.[14]

All along the line the men stayed down, trying to return fire. After the enemy loosed a second volley, "We arose to our feet and again charged upon them," recalled one of the soldiers serving on the left of the regiment, "and as before fell and loaded." At this time the left came under heavy artillery fire. After trying again to press forward, they "fell back to the first ravine in our rear." Here they rallied and prepared to move up again, but soon came under more artillery fire and were ordered back.[15]

With the left retiring, someone in the center mistakenly assumed the whole regiment was falling back, and the order to retreat was given. Thus, after just firing a few rounds, most of the

---

[11] Lieutenant Ira Wood letter, July 23, 1861.

[12] *Ibid.*

[13] *Ibid*; William Petton testimony.

[14] Frank Gates letter, July 23, 1861.

[15] *Ibid.*

men retired from the field – and as it turned out, in great disorder.[16]

While the left and center companies were hastily scrambling for cover in the rear, three companies on the right remained in position. These men stayed where they were, lying down firing at the enemy. In fact, many discharged so many rounds that their muskets became too hot to handle.[17]

During this period, an officer of the 12th recalled that Lieutenant Emory Upton, an aid on General Tyler's staff and a New Yorker who would earn a fine reputation during the war, rode up to the men to give them some words of encouragement.

> The command was given, "cease firing," the boys obeyed and laid there with the balls flying over them, and listened to a pithy little 4th of July speech from Lieut. Upton. [Once finished,] the boys gave him a cheer and resumed their firing.[18]

As the action continued, the companies on the right discovered that the rest of the regiment had fallen back. The officers called a "council of war and concluded we were in a bad fix and had better retire…" Fortunately, it seems that about this time the firing of the enemy was beginning to slacken, and what remained of the 12th ceased fire, gathered their dead and wounded, and headed for the rear.[19]

While the right of the regiment was making their stand, Colonel Walrath was in the rear trying to gather and organize the men of the other companies. Walrath had difficulty trying to rally the men; most had seen enough fighting for the day and fell back fur-

---

[16] Giles Cheseborough testimony; S. C. Anderson testimony. Exactly who ordered the regiment back and how the message was delivered would become a point of controversy. In fact, a captain in the 12th was placed under arrest, apparently by either General Tyler or Colonel Richardson, for supposedly issuing this order to the center of the line. He was later exonerated by a court of inquiry. Syracuse *Courier and Union*, August 14, 1861.

[17] George W. Rowe letter, July 19, 1861; Davis, *Battle at Bull Run*, 120.

[18] Ira Wood letter, July 23, 1861.

[19] *Ibid.*; Retreated in good order, "Ed" letter, July 22, 1861.

Capt. Romeyn Ayres
Later a brigadier
general

Lt. Emory Upton. A staff
officer at First Bull Run.
An innovative brigadier
general later in the war.

Captain Henry A. Barnum
of the 12th New York
Volunteers. Barnum later
served as the colonel of the
149th New York and served
bravely at Gettysburg.
He earned the Congres-
sional Medal of Honor
later in the war while
leading a charge, even
after being wounded.

Photographs from *Miller's Photographic History of the Civil War*

ther. He later stated that their "lack of confidence" in the inferior and unreliable guns they were carrying "was one of the reasons why they would not rally." He remembered some men saying, "Give us rifles, and we will rally."[20]

Colonel Richardson and General Tyler were very displeased with the performance of Walrath and the 12th. Their retiring exposed the left flank of the 1st Massachusetts and they were also then forced back. Tyler's official report of the battle included a harsh censure of the New Yorkers.

> Colonel Richardson having previously given an order for the Twelfth New York to deploy into line and advance into the woods, in an attempt to execute this order the regiment broke, with the exception of two companies, A and I, who stood their ground gallantly, and was only rallied in the woods some mile and a half in the rear. The fire which the regiment encountered was severe, but no excuse for the disorganization it produced.[21]

Although the 12th's performance was far from commendable – except Companies A, E, and I – little blame can be placed on these raw recruits. Later, when given the opportunity to carry effective weapons and receive proper training, these men performed admirably.

While Richardson's brigade was engaging the Confederates, Colonel Sherman's brigade, including the 13th, 69th and 79th New York, was marching from Centerville to provide support. While in town, Sherman's men could hear the cannon and fighting and then received orders to advance (about noon). They double-quicked down the road for about three miles, toward Richardson's rear. As they did, the enemy artillery shells and musket balls began flying around them.

> For the first time in my life I saw cannonballs strike men and crash through trees and saplings above and around us, [wrote General Sherman, after the war] and

---

[20] Colonel E. L. Walrath letter, July 28, 1861.
[21] *O.R..*, Vol. 2, 311. A substantial portion of Co. E was also in position. George W. Rowe letter, July 19, 1861; "Ed" letter, July 22, 1861.

realized the always sickening confusion as one approaches a fight from the rear.[22]

Among the sights was a soldier lying along the road decapitated.[23] A New Yorker under Sherman's command recalled:

> As this was the first time we had been under fire, the experience was somewhat novel – cheering, and even loud talking ceased; men began to look serious – what if one of those shells should hit us? But as shot after shot passed over our heads, or struck the ground on either side without doing any damage, our courage began to mount again.[24]

Another soldier remembered a humorous incident involving Colonel Sherman.

> Colonel Sherman who rode slowly up and down the lines, noticing the men 'ducking' every time a bullet or shell passed over, advised us to "keep cool," adding that there was no use of ducking, for when we heard the sound of the bullets all danger was past. Hardly had these words left his lips, when a big shot or shell came crashing through the trees and but a few feet above him; down went his head close to the pommel of the saddle, and when he raised it again it was to confront a line of grinning faces. "Well, boys," said he, a broad smile softening his rather hard features, *"you may dodge the big ones."*[25]

About the same time that Sherman's brigade was approaching Richardson's position, General McDowell arrived on the scene. He expressed dissatisfaction with Tyler for bringing on this engagement. Later, he informed the general that this action had inter-

---

[22] William T. Sherman, *Memoirs of William T Sherman*. 2 Vols. (New York: 1875).

[23] Todd, *Seventy-Ninth Highlanders*, 24.

[24] A.G.C. letter, July 20, 1861.

[25] Todd, *Seventy-Ninth Highlanders*, 25.

fered with his planned operations. McDowell ordered Tyler to disengage.[26]

With the new orders, the fighting along the front died out. Richardson's and Sherman's troops were ordered back, and as the men retired they picked up blankets and other articles they had discarded in preparation for battle. Also gathered up were the wounded and stragglers, many of whom had fallen out because of the heat.[27] A member of the 13th New York wrote of a particular problem they encountered at this point.

> [When the regiment deployed in support of Richardson's troops] they relieved themselves of their blankets, haversacks, canteens, &c., supposing we were to engage with the enemy at once; but on coming out of the woods, they were all but gone, other soldiers taking them. My coat, blanket, haversack and canteen, could not be found. This left a great many without food or water.[28]

Men of the 13th were not the only ones upset; Colonel Richardson was displeased as well. He was angry at not being allowed to continue the battle and at the performance of the 12th New York.[29] If the 12th had only held their ground, he probably reasoned, then his line could have pushed forward and driven the Confederates back. Their running for the rear not only assured an end to the engagement, but also reflected poorly upon him.

Another concern associated with the 12th retiring was the precedent it established. This was the first major contact with the enemy and some Union troops ran in disorder. "Another issue we discovered [at Blackburn's and Mitchell's Fords]," recalled a New Yorker, "the 'Johnnies' *would fight!* And our dreams of a 'walk over' were dispelled."[30]

---

[26] Davis, *Battle at Bull Run*, 123-24.

[27] *Ibid.*, 124.

[28] A.G.C. letter, July 20, 1861.

[29] Davis, *Battle at Bull Run*, 124.

[30] Todd, *Seventy-Ninth Highlanders*, 25.

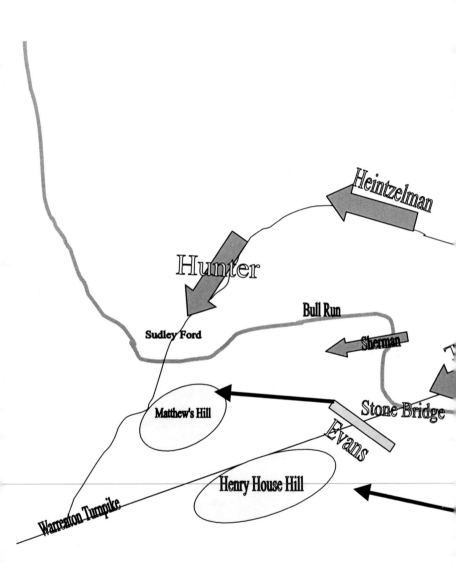

McDowell's march to attack the Confederate left flank at Sudley Ford.

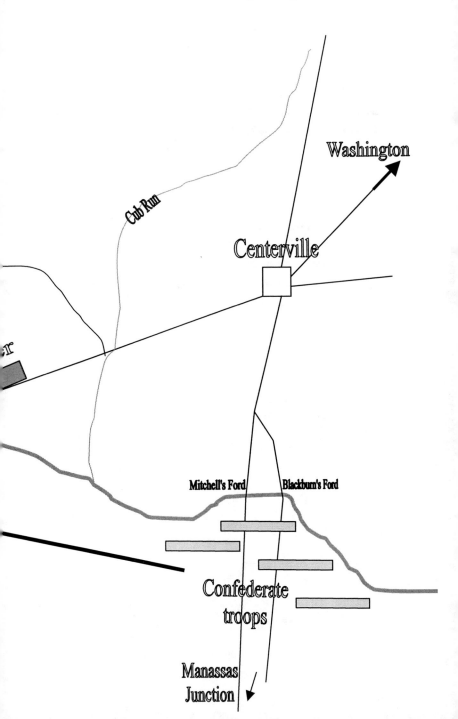

Washington

Cub Run

Centerville

Mitchell's Ford   Blackburn's Ford

Confederate
troops

Manassas
Junction

Chapter Six

"Give it to Them, Boys!"

For the next two days, after the encounter at Blackburn's Ford, McDowell's troops remained in camp at Centerville, while the army was re-supplied and their commander reformulated a plan. Although his idea of trying to outflank the Confederates was sound, turning their right, it turned out, was impractical because of the terrain and strength of the enemy. Now, he would make arrangements to assault Beauregard's left. McDowell hoped to begin his move on the 20th of July, but delays in bringing forward supplies pushed the decisive battle back a day, to July 21st.

During the two days the troops spent in camp, July 19th and 20th, the troops talked, heard many rumors, entertained guests, and even sent some of their number home.

Much of the talk in camp focused on the first encounter between the Federals and Confederates at Blackburn's Ford. A New Yorker remembered one of the former British army soldiers, who was now serving in their ranks, commenting as to his lack of confidence in the volunteers. "Why, a regiment of 'Breetish' soldiers would have gone across that ford and routed the whole 'Secesh' army!" One of his comrades reminded him how a similar volunteer American army defeated the British during the Revolutionary War. "This silenced the croakers."[1]

The sights of the dead and wounded also affected the men. Many of those injured in the skirmish at Blackburn's Ford were cared for in a makeshift hospital nearby and the men saw the wounded and dying being treated. "Here lay the dead body of a boy, not more than eighteen years of age" remembered a New

---

[1] Todd, *Seventy-Ninth Highlanders*, 26.

York soldier near the hospital, "'his mother's hope, his father's joy.' How soon his career was ended!"[2]

Numerous stories now circulated about camp. "The men were excited by all kinds of rumors," a soldier wrote, "and discussed the situation with more anxiety than did generals of later date." One of the more interesting rumors involved a supposed secret weapon.

We are expecting a monster cannon from Washington to-day. It requires 24 horses to draw it, and is to be used for the purpose of throwing barrels of lighted tar and pitch...[3]

Another rumor involved a theme that was particular to this stage of the war. Before the battle, and just afterwards, rumors of rebel atrocities such as bayoneting of Union wounded were common. These stories only ended after many wounded Union prisoners, who were supposedly bayoneted by the Confederates, were returned unharmed after the battle. The following shows the mindset of many of the men concerning this issue, but also reveals insight into their motivations for performing well in the upcoming battle.

These rebels are bound to show us no quarters, and I understand it is the intention of our troops to return the compliment, providing that we can get the cowards out of their masked batteries. The probabilities are, the 13th will have a good chance to convince their friends at home, that they are no 'milk sop' soldiers, but true to their country.[4]

The morale of the Union troops in camp at Centerville was truly a paradoxical issue. While the vast majority of comments in their letters were positive, events, as we shall see, showed that all was not well. Many men previously complaining, such as those in the 13th New York, now seemed positive and confident about the upcoming conflict. "Our rations are salt meat, hard bread, and cof-

---

[2] *Ibid.*, 25-26.

[3] H.H.W. letter, July 19, 1861. Naturally, there was no such weapon.

[4] A.G.C. letter, July 20, 1861.

fee," wrote a man in the 13th, "and there is no grumbling; *everything is fight!*"[5] Unlike the 12th, the 13th had their antiquated weapons replaced before they marched, thus increasing their confidence. The 13th also had the opportunity to see their colonel in action when they came on the battle at Blackburn's Ford. "He is a *soldier*, and our men have the most perfect confidence in him," wrote an officer of the 13th. "He was perfectly cool, and gave his orders [while under fire] as if on dress parade."[6]

Further adding to the confidence of the troops was a rumor circulating about Union successes on other fronts. Stories made their way around camp that General Benjamin Butler's army was advancing on Richmond from the east and General Patterson's force in Harper's Ferry was driving the enemy there (both were false). With this, reasoned a soldier, "All that we had to do was to give Beauregard a thrashing in order to end all the troubles."[7]

Although many of their writings seemed positive, something happened during this period that showed a lack of confidence in victory – several regiments, whose term of enlistment had just expired, turned and walked back to Washington, leaving their comrades to fight the upcoming battle without them.[8] The only New York command leaving was an artillery battery attached to the 8th New York Militia. Demanding their release the loudest was Jimmy Lynch, a politician from New York City and personal friend of the mayor's. They turned their backs not only on their comrades in the army, but also on fellow New Yorkers in the 8th Militia.[9]

Aside from these units leaving, many of the New Yorkers at Centerville saw a "sickening" activity in another command.

A deserter from the regular battalion [attached to Porter's Brigade] was flogged by sentence of court martial, giving the men an opportunity to witness perhaps the last

---

[5] *Ibid.*

[6] H.B. Williams letter, July 19, 1861.

[7] Lewis H. Metcalf, "So Eager Were We All…" *American Heritage*, June 1965, pages 32-41.

[8] Davis, *Battle at Bull Run*, 154; Conyngham, *The Irish Brigade*, 31. General McDowell placed part of the blame on the action (and poor performance of Federal troops) at Blackburn's Ford.

[9] McKay, *The Civil War and New York City*, 89.

sentence of this brutalizing and degrading punishment, as shortly afterward it was forbidden by Congress.[10]

[They were each given thirty lashes] and were then branded, on the side of the hip, with the letter D. It was a sickening sight.[11]

As the time for battle quickly approached, hundreds of civilians began making their way into camp and the surrounding area. Congressmen, senators and other people of influence all came out to see the fight. A New Yorker recalled seeing many influential friends from home; they were "looking finely and enjoying the romance and excitement of the battle field very much."[12]

Amid all the festivity in camp, General McDowell called an officer's conference to prepare for the next day's battle. At 6 P.M. on July 20th, he issued marching orders. Colonel David Hunter's and Colonel Samuel B. Heintzelman's divisions would move off to the Federal right and cross Bull Run near Sudley Springs. This move would threaten Beauregard's left and, unless the defenders moved quickly to counter this action, would place the Union force in the Confederate left rear. As part of this plan, General Tyler's division – less Richardson's Brigade, which was left at Blackburn Ford to distract the Confederates – would approach Bull Run Creek at the Stone Bridge at daybreak. They were to remain there, threatening to cross, until Hunter and Heintzelman's troops appeared. Then they would press forward and assist in driving the enemy.[13]

At 2 A.M. the men were awakened and prepared to advance. Before long things began going wrong for the Federals. Their march was slow and quickly fell behind schedule. A major problem was in sending troops off groping down strange roads in the dark. Further delaying the march was a huge 30-pounder cannon

---

[10] *History of the Fighting Fourteenth*, 226-227.

[11] C.B. Fairchild, *History of the 27th Regiment N. Y. Vols.* (Binghamton, N.Y.: 1888), 10. This writer also mentioned this type of punishment was soon done away with.

[12] Davis, *Battle at Bull Run*, 152; A.G.C. letter, July 20, 1861.

[13] Vincent J. Esposito, ed. *The West Point Atlas of Americans Wars.* Vol. I. 1699-1900. (New York: 1959), Map 21; Davis, *Battle at Bull Run*, 155.

that accompanied the column. Upon reaching a bridge, they held everything up for thirty minutes while trying to get this huge weapon across without collapsing the structure.

Finally, at about 9 A.M., the lead brigade of McDowell's flanking column, Colonel Ambrose Burnside's brigade of Colonel David Hunter's division, approached Sudley Ford. All that stood in the way of Burnside's advance was a small force commanded by Colonel Nathaniel Evans.

"Shanks" Evans was assigned the task of anchoring General Beauregard's left. He placed his force near the Stone Bridge, where General Tyler made demonstrations as if he planned a crossing. Evans watched and became suspicious, however, when Tyler did not press his attack. Then the Southern officer received word of a column approaching further to his left; Evans recognized the threat. Boldly dividing his force, leaving some troops to defend against Tyler, he took a small force to dispute Burnside's advance. He could do little but try to buy some time for Beauregard to send reinforcements.

When the head of Burnside's column emerged from the wooded road near Sudley Ford, Colonel Evans' troops were waiting. The Confederates opened fire, and the battle along Bull Run on July 21, 1861, was begun.[14]

Colonel Hunter, then at the head of Burnside's column, ordered a battery and the 2nd Rhode Island forward, while the remainder of the brigade "formed in a field on the right of the road." The 71st New York Militia, and two artillery pieces attached to their command, were part of Burnside's brigade and soon deployed.[15]

For nearly an hour the Confederates kept Burnside's troops from advancing. Evans' men occupied some woods on Matthew's Hill, overlooking the approach from the ford. During this period Colonel Hunter was wounded, and Burnside assumed tactical control of the fighting. He sent forward another Rhode Island regiment and the 71st New York followed. Colonel Burnside described the action of the 71st.

---

[14] Davis, *Battle at Bull Run*, 171.

[15] *O.R..*, Vol. 2, 395.

Soon after [the 2nd Rhode Island went into action], Colonel [Henry P.] Martin, of the Seventy-first Regiment New York State Militia, led his regiment into action, and planting the two howitzers belonging to the regiment upon the right of his line, worked them most effectively against the enemy's troops.[16]

While the 71st and Burnside's other regiments engaged Evan's forces, Hunter's other brigade, commanded by Colonel Andrew Porter, began filing into line on Burnside's right. Porter's command included the 8th New York State Militia, the 14th Brooklyn, and the 27th New York Volunteers.[17]

The 27th New York was the first regiment to come into line, and they were exhausted from the march.[18]

The distance we traveled [marching to the field] was between fourteen and fifteen miles, and as the day was very warm, we were very tired; but before we reached the scene of action, one of the General's Aids (or the General himself, I don't know which) came to our Colonel and told him there was hot work ahead, and ordered us to take doublequick time. We did so, but when we got on the field, we were so much exhausted that we could hardly stand up.[19]

Another man remembered an incident as they approached the battlefield.

I had one narrow escape. The first ball fired after we went on the ground, came as straight as a line toward me. I stood behind Tom Hilliard. He saw the ball coming and jumped out of the way, and it passed between me and my

---

[16] *Ibid.*, 396.
[17] Davis, *Battle at Bull Run*, 173; *O.R..*, Vol. 2, 315.
[18] *O.R..*, Vol. 2, 391; J.D.M. letter. He believed the march was "between fourteen and fifteen miles."; Fairchild, *History of the 27th*, 11.
[19] J.D.M. letter.

nearest neighbor. This was a cannon-ball, fired before we thought of doing anything.[20]

An officer in the 14th Brooklyn remembered the scene as his men approached the field.

> The Fourteenth marched along an unused railroad grade, and here came the solid shot of the enemy, screeching above and around and, it being the first time under fire, caused many a pale cheek. But determination and resolution were manifest on each countenance and the double quick was taken to the front. Passing through a small wood an opening brought the whole battle-field in view.[21]

As the 14th Brooklyn and 8th New York Militia were emerging from the woods, they were ordered to march down the road past the 27th, which was already forming on Burnside's right. Just as the 27th New York was coming into line, the Confederates launched a counterattack. Major Roberdeau Wheat led his command, the 1st Louisiana Battalion, the "Louisiana Zouaves," toward Burnside's center. At this point the 27th was ordered to charge, to push through the valley in their front and attack the Confederates beyond.[21]

> We made a halt and threw off all our accoutrements excepting canteen and cartridge box, and "sailed in." Our regiment charged down upon a portion of the enemy, and drove them back from a ravine where they were posted. They ran up the hill and joined their comrades, where they made another stand.[22]

---

[20] E.A. letter. The regiment was exposed to artillery fire as they were approaching the field. One man of the 27th was also wounded by a sharpshooter even before the enemy was in sight; he was shot in the foot. Fairchild, *History of the 27th*, 12.

[21] *History of the Fighting Fourteenth*, 228.

[21] Davis, *Battle at Bull Run*, 173; *O.R..*, Vol. 2, 383-384, and 388.

[22] J.D.M. letter.

As the regiment was about to "sail in," a member of the 27th somehow caught his musket on a fence and it discharged, taking off his thumb.[23] An officer in the 27th reported the events as follows:

> [The 27th] formed in line of battle by the left flank on the brow of the hill [beside Burnside's troops] commanding a part of the enemy's position. Without coming to a halt, we were ordered to charge the enemy by a road leading to the valley beneath us, where they were in numbers strongly positioned in and about a large stone house, with a battery of six mounted howitzers commanding the approach. The men, though greatly fatigued and exhausted, gallantly attacked and drove the enemy from the house, who retired in disorder behind their battery, leaving a large number of killed and wounded on the field.[24]

Leading the 27th New York into battle was Colonel Henry Slocum. Born in Delphi, Onondaga County, New York in 1826, young Slocum attended Cazenovia Seminary and then the State Normal School in Albany. Afterwards, he received an appointment to the United States Military Academy and graduated in 1852. While serving in the regular army, he studied and passed the bar exam. Resigning from the service in 1857, he returned to Syracuse and practiced law. In 1859, he was elected to the State Legislature. Slocum was a Republican, "an outspoken anti-slavery man."

At the outbreak of the Civil War, Slocum went to Albany and, as a West Point graduate, offered his services. Governor Morgan asked him to remain in the Capital to assist him, but Slocum instead traveled to Elmira at the invitation of a regiment forming there. Upon arriving, however, he became disillusioned with the unit and refused to accept or pursue the command originally offered, and returned home to Syracuse. But soon the 27th contacted him and offered to make him their commander. He accepted and was unanimously elected their colonel.

Following the battle of Bull Run, Slocum was promoted to brigadier general and eventually rose to major general in com-

---

[23] C.W.M. letter, July 24, 1861; P.M. letter.
[24] *O.R..*, Vol. 2, 388-389.

Colonel Henry W. Slocum of the 27th New York Volunteers.
Slocum is pictured here as a major general, later in the war.

Miller's Photographic History of the Civil War

mand of a corps. He led a corps at Gettysburg and then later in the war served under Sherman in the West and Georgia.[25]

As the 27th prepared to charge, the 14th Brooklyn and 8th New York Militia were coming into action on their right. An officer in the 14th recalled:

> [Upon coming into position,] the men threw off their blankets, which had been carried rolled over their shoulders, and under the lead of Lieutenant Averill, a staff officer of General Porter, the regiment advanced, followed by the Eighth N. G. S. M.... Shot and shell struck and burst around and over the regiment, but from its rapid movement the enemy could not keep the range, and only few men were hurt.[26]

An account of the 8th's participation follows:

> We were then [after emerging from the woods] ordered to advance to a fence a short distance in front; then moved by the right along the road [beyond the 27th]. We here received a destructive fire from the enemy, which caused a temporary break. We ascended the hill, and were called upon by Major Wadsworth, of General McDowell's staff, to charge the woods on our right. Three companies on the right (Captain Burger, Captain Gregory, and Captain Johnson) dashed forward in the woods, dislodging the enemy on the brow of a hill. We here received a fire from the enemy, and returned it. The

---

[25] *New York at Gettysburg*, 1334-1335; Fairchild, *History of the 27th*, 3.

[26] *History of the Fighting Fourteenth*, 228-229. This account is a bit confusing. Colonel Fowler, in describing the events, places the regiment on Henry Hill and near the Dugan house, when most likely he was referring to Matthew's Hill. His description most likely describes events on Matthew's Hill because: 1) he just finished explaining the crossing the Sudley Ford and this was the first action he described. 2) It best fits with the events given by General Porter in his official report. 3) It best fits the accounts given by other commands such as the 8th and 27th New York.

fire now became so hot that the men were ordered to fall back in the woods.[27]

Apparently, at this point several regiments from Porter's and Burnside's command reached the brow of Matthew's Hill. Now, there was much confusion on the field. Not only were the commands becoming separated, but because each side had units in gray and blue uniforms, the identities of approaching regiments were not certain. Additionally, more Confederate reinforcements were arriving on the scene. The following describes a nearly disastrous encounter of the 27th New York.

> ...our ranks, which had been thrown into some disorder, were ordered to reform [after the charge up the hill]; but before the order could be executed, we saw two regiments coming, at double quick, over the crest of the hill from our rear and left, – a direction from which we did not expect the enemy. They were dressed in gray, and we mistook them for the 8th New York [who wore gray uniforms]. As they moved around in our front, some of the men called out "that they were enemies," and began to fire. Others, excitedly "declared them to be the 8th New York," and begged us not to fire on our own men. Just then a Confederate straggler between the lines, ran up to Col. Slocum, and declared that the "regiment yonder wanted to surrender." Slocum threatened the man with drawn sword, but he persisted; and, by the Colonel's order, Adjutant Jenkins started towards the enemy, waving a Havelock as a flag of truce. "What regiment are you?" he asked. He was answered by the unfurling of the Confederate colors and the firing of a volley. He rode back to our lines, exclaiming, "Give it to them, boys!" The 27th responded, firing at will, but many did not hear him, and still held their fire. Our mistake had given them time to form in line of battle, under cover of thick bushes, and they poured volley after volley into us, with deadly effect. Our men replied vigorously, but could not long

---

[27] *O.R.*., Vol. 2, 387-388.

stand under such a fire, and began to retire slowly over the crest of the hill.[28]

A member of the 27th, who had earlier dropped from exhaustion, now came running toward the regiment. As he did, he recalled:

I met Lieut. Col. Chambers galloping back to get help for our regiment, and he rushed up to one of the field officers ... and called for aid, for heaven's sake, to relieve our boys. He said the boys were surrounded [by the enemy]. When I heard this I ran down to the woods and found our regiment retreating, carrying back our Col. [Henry Slocum], wounded in the thigh with several of our [regiment wounded and killed... Now] we made a stand, the balls of the artillery and musketry whirling over our heads in a perfect storm. Our Major [Joseph Bartlett] took command... [29]

Major Bartlett described the fight.

We were now engaged by more than twice our own numbers, and fired upon from concealed positions, and receiving the fire of the battery from its new point of attack. Perceiving the necessity of support, I rallied about 200 of the Eighth New York Regiment on the brow of the hill commanding the enemy, and the colonel withdrew the regiment to the top of the hill in a perfectly exhausted condition, formed, and marched them into the woods for rest. [Slocum was wounded during this withdrawal].[30]

To this point, the battle was a gradual escalation of fighting as both sides sent in reinforcements around Matthew's Hill. With the appearance of more Confederate troops, such as those that drove back the 27th, the battle was temporarily shifting in favor of the Southerners.

---

[28] Fairchild, *History of the 27th*, 12-13.
[29] J.A. Copeland letter, July 24, 1861.
[30] *O.R..*, Vol. 2, 388-389.

Chapter Seven

"Our Hurrahs Were Premature"

Around 10:00 o'clock in the morning, the Confederates still maintained a strong presence on Matthew's Hill. Colonel Nathan Evans' battered command had much fight left in it, but their numbers were greatly diminished. General Bernard Bee and Colonel Francis Bartow brought their brigades into position supporting Evans. These three Confederate commands, in a desperate effort to buy more time – seeing more Union reinforcements on the way – advanced against Porter's and Burnside's brigades. This was probably part of what the 27th New York had faced.

It seems that the 14th Brooklyn was also involved in defending against this attack.

From the woods on the far side of the road we received a severe and continuous fire of musketry from a force of the enemy in ambush, who could not be seen. The regiment returned the fire, then broke and reformed behind the fence of the road. At this time an officer of Griffin's battery made an appeal to the regiment to go to the support of the battery or it would be lost. And Lieutenant Averill, riding up, gave the order to the regiment, and it formed behind the battery, which then changed its position. As the conspicuous uniform of the regiment attracted the fire of the enemy, it was advanced to a position some one hundred yards in front of Griffin's battery and ordered to lie down in line of battle. The enemy's fire followed the regiment, and thus the battery was relieved of it.[1]

During this part of the battle, the 8th, 14th and 27th New York regiments were particularly battered. Colonel Porter wrote in his report, "The Fourteenth, though it had broken, [in the action described above] was soon rallied in rear of Griffin's battery..." And, "The Eighth had lost its organization." Additionally, as we saw, the 27th not only lost their commander, but also suffered casualties, coming through a tough fight that thinned their ranks.[2]

While Burnside and Porter's Brigades were repelling the Confederate counterattack, another Federal division was coming into position to reinforce them. Colonel Samuel Heintzelman's two brigades followed Hunter's across Sudley Ford, and now approached Matthew's Hill, preparing to deploy and extend Burnside's line toward Bull Run.

Heintzelman's command, totaling seven regiments, included two from New York: the 11th New York "Fire Zouaves" and the 38th New York Volunteers, both primarily formed in New York City. The appearance of Heintzelman's command was too much for the Confederates; they realized they would have to abandon Matthew's Hill.

Moving quickly toward the front, the soldiers in the 11th New York heard shouts to hurry forward; the enemy was driving them back. Heintzelman's troops were ordered to move at "Double-quick" time to the front. A member of the 11th remembered how difficult it was to maintain order at this pace, especially for troops with limited training. He compared seeing a well-drilled unit moving at double quick in Washington and then how his command attempted to do the same on the field of battle.

---

[1] *History of the Fighting Fourteenth*, 229.
[2] *O.R..*, Vol. 2, 384; Also see Davis, *Battle at Bull Run*, 182. "The initial encounters between Hunter's brigades and Evans had left at least two of the Federal regiments, the 8th and 14th New York, seriously demoralized." The 14th recovered and fought on, the 8th was basically out of action, and although the 27th reformed, most of the unit did little more than maintain a position in support for the rest of the battle. Fairchild, *History of the 27th*, 12. Also see Davis, *Battle at Bull Run*, 192.

I remember one day to have seen the Massachusetts' 5th coming down Pennsylvania Avenue at double quick with drums beating to keep the proper time, and it looked very well. But with our regiment, it was another matter, and performed in a manner not set down in our tactics. Anyone who has seen a closely contested race between two fire engine companies down Grand Street can form a good idea of what double quick was with us.[3]

Heintzelman's command was not the only Federal force approaching the contested hill. Colonel William Sherman's brigade, including the 13th, 69th and 79th New York, was also moving toward the location, but coming in from the rear of the Confederate line.

As part of General Tyler's division, they were waiting near the Stone Bridge for the approach of Hunter's and Heintzelman's divisions. This would signal their push across Bull Run to reinforce the Federal effort. Fortunately for the Federals, in the time spent waiting for Hunter's division to advance, Colonel Sherman took it upon himself to find an alternate route for crossing the stream, just in case things did not go as planned. Now, with Hunter's advance stalled on Matthew's Hill, orders came for Tyler to press ahead. While the Confederates still maintained a force to dispute their crossing at the Stone Bridge, Sherman took his brigade upstream, toward Matthew's Hill, and crossed unopposed.[4]

Earlier that morning, Sherman's troops could hear the fighting off toward Matthew's Hill and wondered what was happening. Some climbed trees in an attempt to catch a glimpse of the battle, while most restlessly waited for orders to move.[5] Now these men excitedly headed toward the battle.

Colonel Sherman led the 69th New York off toward the point he found – they were the first of his four regiments to cross the stream. Ironically, although they would soon prove themselves among the fiercest fighters on the field, they were not anxious to

---

[3] Metcalf, "So Eager Were We All…"

[4] Davis, *Battle at Bull Run*, 164; *West Point Atlas of Americans Wars*, Map 22.

[5] Todd, *Seventy-Ninth Highlanders*, 31.

enter the fray with wet feet. Here is how members of another unit described the crossing.

The 13th stripped off all their blankets, &c, and marched on in the double quick, through the woods and fields of grain, till we came to the stream called Bull's Run – a nasty, filthy creek at the foot of a very steep rocky hill, about 25 feet wide and three feet deep. Here the 69th were detained somewhat, notwithstanding the exhortations of officers to dash through it. The 13th went through it with a hop, skip and jump movement.[6]

[Although the 69th proved to be brave fighters on the field, they] "tip toed" it through the stream, on a few scattered stones, notwithstanding the strong entreaties of their officers to "push on," to "advance;" and not till the cry came that "the enemy was retreating," did they advance up the hill with any vigor![7]

Once across the stream, Sherman's troops entered some woods and marched until out in the open, a half mile north of the Warrenton Road. This placed his command in the right rear of the Confederates preparing to fall back from Matthew's Hill. In fact, seeing troops approaching from this direction, the Southerners at first believed them to be reinforcements. A Confederate unit, the 4th Alabama, actually moved to reform their line behind Sherman's men. But when the 69th saw their colors, they opened fire. It was during this period that the Irishmen lost their lieutenant colonel.[8] Here is how Colonel Sherman and the officers in the 69th reported the incident.

Lieutenant-Colonel Haggerty, of the Sixty-ninth, without orders, rode out and endeavored to intercept their retreat. One of the enemy, in full view, at short range, shot Haggerty, and he fell dead from his horse.[9]

---

[6] A.G.C. letter, July 22, 1861.

[7] *Ibid.*, July 30, 1861.

[8] Davis, *Battle at Bull Run*, 185-187.

[9] *O.R..*, Vol. 2, 369.

Lieutenant Colonel Haggerty was killed by a Louisiana zouave, whom he pursued as the latter was on his retreat with his regiment into the woods, and several of our men were severely wounded.[10]

Seeing their lieutenant colonel fall, the 69th opened fire on the enemy troops in their front. Soon, the Confederates passed beyond their range, off toward Henry House Hill.

By this time Southern troops were trying to reform on the next ridge, some making a stand in the valley between Matthew's and Henry Hills. Sherman ordered his brigade to continue on toward Matthew's Hill, where General McDowell was seen trying to organize his forces. McDowell rode up to Sherman's brigade as they approached.

"[W]e formed in front of the Carter house, on the brow of the hill overlooking the valley of Young's Branch," recalled a member of the 79th New York Highlanders. "Just as we halted, McDowell and his staff rode down the lines, waving their caps and shouting, 'Victory! Victory! The day is ours!'" A member of the 79th reportedly stepped forward and asked the general to send them in, "before they all run away!" A former British soldier in the ranks, grabbed the naïve lad and told him to be quiet, assuring him he would see all the fighting he wanted by the end of the day.[11]

Seeing the enemy troops retiring, McDowell ordered Sherman's fresh brigade in pursuit. The colonel turned and shouted orders.[12] Sherman described the advance.

Placing Colonel Quinby's regiment [13th New York] in front, in column by divisions, I directed the other regiments to follow in line of battle, in the order of the Wisconsin Second, New York Seventy-ninth, and New York Sixty-ninth. Quinby's regiment advanced steadily down the hill and up the ridge, from which he opened fire upon the enemy, who made another stand on ground very

---

[10] *Ibid.*, 371.

[11] Todd, *Seventy-Ninth Highlanders*, 34.

[12] Davis, *Battle at Bull Run*, 186; Todd, *Seventy-Ninth Highlanders*, 35.

favorable to him, and the regiment continued advancing as the enemy gave way…[13]

Colonel Quinby dismounted and led his regiment of just over 600 men forward.[14] Isaac Quinby graduated from West Point in 1843, and then served as a 2nd lieutenant in the artillery. He fought in the war against Mexico, with Bragg's Battery. In the years following, he taught at West Point, after which, he resigned and accepted an appointment to teach at the University of Rochester, where he was for nine years previous to the outbreak of the Civil War. A good commander, Quinby had the confidence of his men.[15]

The following are some descriptions of the events, given by two members of the 13th.

Soon General McDowell rode along the line, waving his glove. He appeared to think that the day was won. Soon, however, new batteries were opened on us. The 13th marched down across the field in front of one of these batteries while it was raining death over the field. Soon the balls came in among us. At my right a dull, heavy sound was heard. I looked around; a poor man was being carried off dead or wounded. Soon another shot struck the 13th on my left.[16]

There [on Matthew's Hill] Generals McDowell and Sherman met, and congratulated each other, shaking hands under a general hurrah.

Alas! Their rejoicing and our hurrahs were premature. The order to advance was given. – Our regiments, though exhausted by marching since 2 [A.M.], in terrible heat, stimulated by the flush of victory, went down the hill and climbed the next height. On its top we came within range

---

[13] *O.R..*, Vol. 2, 369.

[14] William H. Benjamin account; Cazeau, *Account of the Thirteenth New York*, 2; Rochester *Democrat and American*, July 26, 1861. States less than 650 men.

[15] Colonel Isaac Quinby biography: Rochester *Democrat and American*, May 14, 1861.

[16] Ensign Gilbert letter, July 27, 1861.

of the main battery of the enemy, and the balls began to fly round our heads like hail....

Under a hail storm of bullets and grapeshot, by which quite a number out of our regiment fell, we marched to a small hill on the left, where we took position. The several [companies] of our regiment took their turn in marching to the crest, and firing down upon the enemy. Finally, some of our artillery was planted on the hill above us, and we had the pleasure of receiving most of the bullets destined for them.[17]

It seems that while in line here, supporting the battery, part or all of the 13th helped fight off a charge made by the "Louisiana Zouaves."

I have reason to think the Louisiana 'Tigers' – Jeff Davis' pet lambs – will long remember the New York 13th. We were ordered to support Sherman's battery, and came upon the 'Tigers,' who, it seems (according to one of them, who was taken prisoner) were chosen to storm this famous battery, and capture it at all hazards. But our faithful rifles and the quick steady movement of our boys, cut them up dreadfully.[18]

Meanwhile, Sherman's other regiments filed into the Warrenton Road, where a slight depression helped protect them from increasing artillery fire. They followed this to their right, and remained here waiting for developments – That is, McDowell to organize an attack.[20]

---

[17] Anonymous, German soldier in the 13th New York, July 23, 1861. This account matches statements in the official reports. "...Quinby's regiment occupied another ridge to our left..." Sherman's report, *O.R.*, Vol. 2, 369 and 370.

[18] A.G.C. letter, July 30, 1861; Another man recalled their time protecting the battery. "We took our position behind the battery, and held it till the battery was withdrawn – lying down all the while – still losing a few men, and pecking down a few with our rifles." S.A.M. letter, July 23, 1861.

[20] *O.R..*, Vol. 2, 369.

While in this position, the regiments were exposed to artillery fire. Under cover of the embankment, the Color bearer for the 69th was waving his regimental flag defiantly, thus drawing even more attention from the Confederate artillery. Colonel Corcoran rode over to the color guard and instructed that the flags be lowered. "Don't ask me, colonel," one bearer replied, "I'll never lower it." Just then an artillery projectile found its mark and the man was killed. Another grabbed the banner and soon met the same fate. Presumably with this lesson learned, the bearers then lowered their cherished banners.[21]

The artillery fire was heavy along the whole line at this point. Even back on Matthew's Hill, the 27th New York once again advanced to a supporting position near the stone house, and received fire.[22]

> The cannon balls and shells flew over our heads like flashes of lightening, we could distinctly hear a ball from the moment it started till it struck the ground; when it would often bound fifty feet into the air. Some passed within two feet of my head when lying on my face under a small bank for protection from their batteries.[23]

> The enemy fired so quick and fast it came like hail – bombs, shells, grape-shot, cannon-balls, and rifle-balls. We had to lie down under a bank; but they saw us there and fired quicker yet. I was lying by a man when a cannon-ball struck him in the stomach and tore him all to pieces.[24]

Before long, the artillery firing along the line subsided. At this point a temporary lull settled over the field while each side brought up reinforcements. Within an hour, McDowell would begin the next phase of his attack – the effort to drive the Confederates from Henry House Hill.

---

[21] Conyngham, *The Irish Brigade*, 41.

[22] Fairchild, *History of the 27th*, 13; *O.R.*, Vol. 2, 384.

[23] C.B. letter, July 24, 1861.

[24] P.M. letter.

Chapter Eight

"Leaving it a Perfect Wreck"

Although General Beauregard expected McDowell's main attack to come much further to the east, near Mitchell's Ford, he was becoming increasingly aware that his left was in jeopardy. Thanks to the incredible efforts of his subordinates, mainly Evans, Bee, and Bernard, he was afforded precious time to start funneling troops to the threatened area. Aside from Bee's and Bernard's commands, Thomas Jackson's Virginia Brigade was now on the field, along with Wade Hampton's Legion.

Overall Confederate commander General Joseph E. Johnston was also on the scene. He was not pleased with Beauregard's delay in shifting troops to the left. Johnston spurred Beauregard's efforts, and soon more brigades were headed toward McDowell's forces.[1]

Sometime around 2:00, while more Confederate brigades were arriving, General McDowell began his push to carry Henry House Hill. A major part of the effort would be his advancing two batteries ahead of the line, to soften the Southern defenses – much as Napoleon used to do. This, however, would prove to be a serious mistake.

General McDowell ordered Colonel Heintzelman to send forward some artillery with infantry to support them. Heintzelman called forward two of his New York regiments, the 11th and 38th Volunteers. The 14th Brooklyn, now reformed and prepared for more fighting, would soon follow.

When the 11th New York Zouaves arrived near Matthew's Hill, they were tired and out of breath. Soon after crossing Bull

---

[1] Davis, *First Blood*, 136.

Run, they dropped their knapsacks and double quicked toward the front. Originally sent to support the defensive line, they received orders to advance with the batteries. A member of the unit recalled that this was when the "pet lambs [were] led to slaughter."[2]

The condition of these troops about to enter the battle was not good. They were tired. One recalled they just wanted five minutes rest to catch their breath.[3] A New York soldier who entered the field in the same condition wrote:

> The fact is that we were whipped before we reached the field, after so long a march, without anything to eat, and nothing to drink but water so thick that it would scarcely drop [from puddles], you may believe that we were not in a very good condition to fight.[4]

The 38th was in little better shape when ordered to the front. An officer in the regiment recalled their activities before being sent forward.

> We followed the battery in line, dressing on our colors. We went on double quick time for about one mile. When we got within half a mile of the position to be occupied by the battery on an eminence, cannon shot and bombs went whizzing by and over our heads at the rate of 12 a minute. *I took out my watch and counted them.* Before we had come to a halt [probably on Matthew's Hill] we had to cross three fences. After we got in range of their batteries, I never saw a rifled gun pointed more accurately than they pointed their rifled cannon. Our battery was soon unable to sustain the awful fire to which it was exposed. We were then ordered to follow and support another battery on a hill, three-fourths of a mile on our right.[5]

---

[2] Davis, *Battle at Bull Run*, 184. "Pet lambs" refers to the units who received special attention and favor with the media and, as some claimed, from the government itself.

[3] Metcalf, "So Eager Were We All…"

[4] C.W.M. letter, July 24, 1861.

[5] Capt. W.H. Baird letter, July 23, 1861.

General McDowell sent word to his chief of artillery, Major William Barry; it was time to send the artillery forward. Captain Charles Griffin would lead his five pieces and Captain J. B. Ricketts would command another six. Upon hearing the plan, Griffin protested. Henry Hill was no place for isolated batteries. Barry assured the captain he would have infantry support, but the artilleryman had no confidence in the ninety-day recruits. "I will go," said Griffin, "but mark my words, they will not support us."[5]

Griffin's and Rickett's guns started across the valley between the two hills then up the Henry Hill slope. Eleven guns dropped trail within 300 yards of the Confederate lines and opened fire. As the batteries advanced, Major Barry went back to lead the 11th and 14th New York regiments forward.[6] In the meantime, the 38th was already following the guns to the hill.

Commanding the 38th New York Volunteers was Colonel Hobart Ward. Born in New York City in 1823, Ward's family had a tradition of fighting for their country – his grandfather fought in the American Revolution while his father defended the country during the War of 1812. As a young man Ward had enlisted in the army, serving as a sergeant during the war with Mexico. Sometime after the war, he left the service and worked as a municipal employee in New York City. Following Fort Sumter he offered his services and helped raise the 38th Volunteers. Because of his leadership and prior military experience, he was given command of the regiment.[7]

Unfortunately, this was not Ward's best day. In fact, the 38th was having problems as far as the physical health of their commanders was concerned, of which a member of the regiment wrote:

> Our Col. was weak with the heat and fatigue of the march, being so sick when we left camp that he could not keep his seat in the saddle; our Lieut. Colonel was covered with boils, but he kept the field on foot; being unable

---

[5] Davis, *Battle of Bull Run*, 204.

[6] Davis, *First Blood*, 143.

[7] Fox, *New York at Gettysburg*, 1356.

Colonel Hobart Ward of the 38th New York.
Pictured here as a brigadier general later in the war.

Miller's Photographic History of the Civil War

to ride; [And soon after being under fire] our Major was struck by a ball near the ankle...[8]

Oddly, the commander of the 11th New York, Lieutenant Colonel N. L. Farnham, had also been ill, only joining his troops on the march that morning. Farnham's Fire Zouaves followed Major Barry to the front, somewhere off to the right of the Federal batteries. Coming into position, two of the 11th's companies were detached and left in the rear as a reserve.[9]

The 11th New York was a very conspicuous regiment on the field. Aside from their flashy uniforms, they were also distinguishable by their size, over a thousand men. A fellow New York soldier commented at the time, "The Ellsworth Zouaves went on the field with 1,100 of the bravest fellows that ever lived."[10] Their bravery was about to be severely tested.

Watching the approach of the zouaves were men belonging to Thomas Jackson's Brigade. Jackson was earlier in the day heralded for standing like a "stone wall" in the face of heavy fire. Now his men prepared to deliver some deadly fire of their own.

When the 11th reached the top of the hill, the Virginians let loose a volley. Muskets flashed from the "woods in front" of the zouaves and from the "spur of dwarf pines and bushes" on their right. Their colonel yelled, "Down, every one of you." Flopping to the ground just as the Confederates unleashed a second volley, the men listened to the thunder of the rebel muskets and to the bullets zipping past overhead. The zouaves now began popping up to discharge their weapons toward the "unseen enemy" in the woods and bushes, dropping again to reload.[11]

A member of a Massachusetts regiment watching the action wrote:

---

[8] Capt. W.H. Baird letter, July 23, 1861. (Confirmed in the John H. Morrison letter, July 23, 1861 and *O.R.*, Vol. 2, 414.)

[9] Metcalf, "So Eager Were We All..."; Willcox's report. *O.R.*, Vol. 2, 408; There were 350 Marines in action, but they were raw recruits just like the other regiments. See *O.R.*., Vol. 2, 392.

[10] C.B. letter, July 24, 1861.

[11] Metcalf, "So Eager Were We All..."

The Zouaves stood their ground, firing in lines, then falling on their faces to load. Their ranks were becoming thinned, yet they would not retire.[12]

A battalion of Marines was also in line with the 11th and their situation was not much better. Order in the two regiments was fast deteriorating. Frustrated with being caught in the open, some Fire Zouaves started crawling toward the wood line, apparently to get a better shot at the enemy. Others, especially on the right, began falling back in disorder. Adding to the increasing stream of soldiers heading to the rear were friends carrying wounded comrades to safety. This was a problem at this point in the war; later battles would see orders issued forbidding leaving your place in line to help the wounded. Each bullet wounding a soldier removed two muskets from the field – the wounded man and someone to assist him to safety in the rear.[13]

Soon, it appears, the right of the 11th was driven back down the hill. A soldier remembered falling back, but seeing the rest of his regiment still on the field in front. Before long this fire was too much for the men and they began to retire. A witness recalled:

> The Fire Zouaves advanced in line boldly up that hill, across Sudley Ford road, and up towards the stunted pines at its summit, but soon, together with the Marines, they came running back in disorder. This was the last of the Fire Zouaves, they never rallied again, except in part…[14]

While this seems an exaggeration, it does show that much of the order in the 11th was lost. Now the 14th Brooklyn entered the fray.

> Now came the earnest work of the Fourteenth. By the stampeding of the Fire Zouaves, and other causes, the batteries were lost, half their men shot down, and not horses enough left to draw off the guns. General

---

[12] Edward S. Barrett letter. *Voices of the Civil War: First Manassas*, 131.

[13] Metcalf, "So Eager Were We All…"; Davis, *Battle at Bull Run*, 209.

[14] *History of the Fighting Fourteenth*, 229.

Battle for Henry House Hill

During the later part of the afternoon, the battle focused on the control of Henry House Hill and the Federal artillery pieces there. Attacks and counterattacks were launched, but finally the Federal right gave way, initiating a dramatic Union retreat.

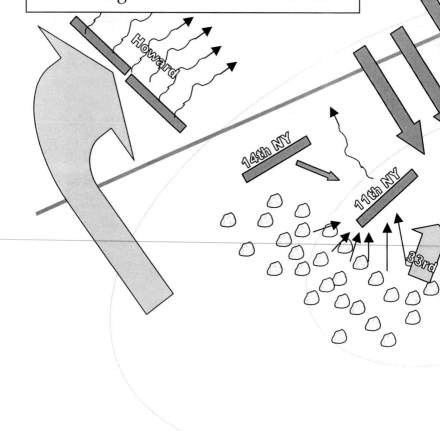

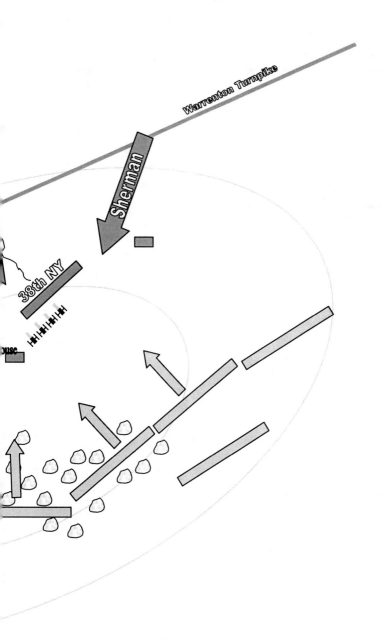

McDowell in person directed the movements of the Fourteenth up that hill, assisted by Lieutenant Averill. After starting up in line the general ordered a change of direction by the flank, which was executed. Lieutenant Averill, with the consent of the general, ordered another change of direction by an advance in line again, which carried the regiment to a position near the woods on the right of the lost batteries. In going up, the regiment passed the Fire Zouaves and Marines coming back in disorder.

The Fourteenth advanced to within forty yards of the enemy's infantry, who were advancing up a ravine, or water course, only the upper part of their bodies being visible, in column by division. The fire of the Fourteenth was directed on their leading division with terrible effect, nearly the entire division being cut down. They quickly deployed and opened fire. While in this position, General Wadsworth, then a volunteer major on General McDowell's staff, by coolly sitting on his horse and discharging the contents of his revolver at the foe in the presence of and near the regiment, [gained our admiration]....

The fire from the front, together with a crossfire from the bushes on the right and the shot and shells from the batteries made the position so hot that the regiment was soon forced to fall back.[15]

While the 14th and 11th were under fire on the slope and beginning to fall back, Confederate cavalry commander J.E.B. Stuart ordered a charge. The aggressive Stuart had just arrived on the field and looked for an opportunity to engage the enemy. Upon getting confirmation that those on his front were not Wheat's Zouaves – the Louisiana "Tigers" – he ordered his cavalry forward. The horsemen thundered toward the flank of the red-legged 14th Brooklyn and the 11th New York zouaves beyond.[16]

Sabers and bayonets flashed as muskets discharged, emptying saddles. The two reserve companies of the 11th, and those from the right of the regiment previously fallen back, helped scatter Stuart's

[15] *History of the Fighting Fourteenth*, 229-230.
[16] Davis, *Battle at Bull Run*, 207.

14th Brooklyn   11th New York Fire Zouaves

Drawings from *Battles and Leaders of the Civil War*

cavalry, but the brave charge disrupted what order was left in the units. Colonel Farnham of the 11th was mortally wounded in the melee.[17]

At this point, the situation for the Federals went from bad to worse. On the top of the hill one of Jackson's regiments, the 33rd Virginia, dressed in blue, was approaching the Federal batteries, now unsupported on their right.

When the 33rd Virginia stepped out into the open, Captain Griffin immediately turned his guns and prepared to fire. Major Barry, however, insisted these troops were Union reinforcements and he should hold his fire. Griffin protested, but to no avail. The Virginians advanced, leveled their muskets and fired. This volley effectively ended Griffin's battery as a fighting force.

Some members of the 11th and the Marines had reformed and tried to aid the artillerymen. An officer from the battery approached the Fire Zouaves and yelled, "For God's sake, boys, save my battery." A collected mass of the zouaves formed and dashed up the hill toward the abandoned guns, but they were driven back. Their effort was heroic, but unsuccessful.[18]

On the other end of the line, to the left of the batteries, the 38th was also under heavy fire. Here are two descriptions of their action:

> Advancing by the flank under a galling fire, the regiment was halted within supporting distance of Griffin's battery, which had now opened upon the enemy, and properly formed to resist a threatened attack from the enemy's cavalry and infantry, which had shown themselves in large numbers on the borders of a grove to the right and front. In this position my regiment, under a spiteful and destructive fire from the enemy's batteries, remained until forced to retire, and its presence not being deemed requisite because of the fact that Griffin's battery had been compelled to leave the field.[19]

---

[17] Harrison H. Comings letter, *Voices of the Civil War: First Manassas,* 128.

[18] Metcalf, "So Eager Were We All…"; Davis, *Battle at Bull Run,* 212.

[19] *O.R..,* Vol. 2, 414.

Charge of the 11th New York Fire Zouaves. Drawing from *Battles and Leaders of the Civil War*

We scarcely reached [Henry Hill], going the entire distance through a shower of musketry, heavy shot and shell, when our battery was knocked all to pieces by a shot from a rifled cannon, which struck a wheel of a gun carriage, killed one gunner and took off the leg from another, and killed two horses, leaving it a perfect wreck. We were lying behind a rail fence some ten yards in rear of the battery, ready to support it from a charge of the enemy's cavalry. By this time, however, the rebels made a charge on another gun [battery] at our right. – They came out of the woods in front of us. – We were unsupported, the Fire Zouaves were the nearest regiment to us [but they were already forced back]... We met the rebels in between and in front of the gun they were trying to capture, and pen cannot describe the awful scene that followed. Musket balls went through and through our ranks by the hundreds. As we were unsupported, and the enemy had about 1,000 to our 688, we were compelled to fall back, which we did in tolerable order.[20]

Now the final stage of the battle was ready to play out. The Federals and Confederates would fight over this small hill and possession of the abandoned guns. For nearly two hours both sides would attack and counterattack, hoping to gain control of this key position.[21]

---

[20] Capt. W.H. Baird letter, July 23, 1861.
[21] Davis, *Battle at Bull Run*, 214.

Chapter Nine

"Fear of Being Called

a Coward"

The attack of the 33rd Virginia and the subsequent counterattack by the Fire Zouaves and Marines, along with the defensive stand of the 38th and other regiments, resulted in at least four of Griffin's guns being left on the hill, with neither side in possession of them. While regiments from Hampton's Legion and Jackson's Brigade approached the abandoned cannons, Colonel William Franklin and Colonel Orlando Willcox led portions of their Union brigades up the slope to recover the pieces.[1] It appears that the 38th New York was part of this force. Here are two descriptions of the action by members of the 38th.

> [After] retiring to a road about one hundred yards distant [from their original position on the hill], my regiment was again formed in line of battle, and under the eye of the commander-in-chief, General McDowell, the men, inspired by his presence upon the field and led by [Colonel Ward], it dashed gallantly up the hill towards a point where Rickett's battery had been abandoned....
>
> Before arriving at the brow of the hill we met the enemy in large force; one of his infantry regiments, apparently fresh upon the field, advancing steadily towards us in line of battle. A large number of the men of this regi-

---

[1] Davis, *Battle at Bull Run*, 216.

ment had advanced in front of their line, and had taken possession of Rickett's battery, and were endeavoring to turn the guns upon us. A well-directed and destructive fire was immediately opened upon the enemy by my regiment and a portion of another that had rallied on our left (I think the Fourteenth New York State Militia), and after a sharp conflict he was forced to retreat in disorder and with great loss, seeking shelter in the woods from whence he had previously emerged.

The enemy not succeeding in taking with him Rickett's battery, which seemed to have been the chief object of his attack, it fell into the hands of my regiment, by whom three of its guns were dragged a distance of three hundred yards, and left in a road, apparently out of reach of the enemy. Another rally was then again made by my regiment, the gallant men readily responding to the orders of their officers. Advancing in double-quick time to the right and front towards a dense woods, in which the enemy had been concealed in large force...my regiment, with detached portions of others of our force, became engaged in a sharp and spirited skirmish with the enemy's infantry...[2]

[During the charge] Our flag was carried to the center of the regiment. It dropped, some of the enemy started to get it. Byron Stevens started for it, but it was got by one of our regiment before he reached it.... We rallied three times and drove the enemy back to the woods. Never were muskets pointed with more deadly effect. They went down before us like grass before the mower; around one gun they were piled in heaps....

We drove them into the woods again where they had breastworks that could not be taken. We halted and poured volley after volley in upon them. Their firing ceased for about 3 minutes, when they formed behind their breastworks and opened it again. Had they fired with as much certainty as our men did, they would have

---

[2] *O.R.*, Vol. 2, 414.

swept our whole regiment completely away. – The balls flew in and around us like hail.[3]

The following excerpt from a member of the 38th to his father gives an interesting perspective of how hot the fire was and a strange calmness many experienced in combat.

While we stood there [on the top of the hill exposed to fire from the woods], I was wondering all the while that a ball did not hit me; *but I got off without a scratch!* Why I saw men fall all around me. Some had their head shot off clean from the body; some had both legs and arms taken off and others fell with balls in their heads. It was one continual *whiz* around my head. Men would drop next to me; but although I always thought I would feel a little fear on entering a field of battle, yet I was never more cool and steady in my life, notwithstanding the hot weather and fatigue.[4]

Some evidence suggests that this effort took place in conjunction with a counterattack launched by part of the 11th New York.[5] This could be the effort previously described, but probably was another attempt launched by a group of Fire Zouaves and at least a portion of the 27th New York to recover the batteries. A member of the 27th described an attack up the slope in front of where a Confederate battery came into position.

Our company and the Fire Zouaves marched up to take one of the masked batteries, and stood there and fought until we were ordered to retreat. The bullets rattled

[3] Capt. W.H. Baird letter, July 23, 1861.

[4] John. H. Morrison letter, July 23, 1861.

[5] Descriptions of the counterattack launched by the 38th suggest the presence of the 11th New York as well as the 14th Brooklyn. Capt. W.H. Baird letter, July 23, 1861; John. H. Morrison letter, July 23, 1861; *O.R..*, Vol. 2, 414. Rallying, the 11th and others probably advanced on the left of the 38th, away from the woods.

around my head like rain. I can't see now how I was so lucky as to come out all right.[6]

Along with the 38th and the other units mentioned, Colonel Franklin's 5th and 11th Massachusetts, and Colonel Willcox's 1st Michigan and 1st Minnesota were also part of the effort to regain the hill. Colonel Samuel Heintzelman, the commander of the Third Division, personally led some of these units forward.

Heintzelman stated in his report that after the cavalry melee in the rear of the 11th New York was over, he personally began directing troops into position. He saw the 1st Minnesota and led them forward to the hill, where they also were repulsed, but fell back in good order. The 1st Michigan advanced, but met with the same fate. The 14th Brooklyn then reformed, most likely after rallying from their earlier advance, and Heintzelman led them up the slope, to the left. The colonel does not give a flattering account of their action, stating, "they broke and ran."[7] This was probably the event a member of the 14th described below:

The regiment... advanced again to the summit. This time it was supported by the battalion of Marines in its rear. On reaching the top of the hill, as the enemy's volley came belching forth, the men, without command, dropped to the ground, and the shots passed over them and took effect upon the Marines in their rear, who, notwithstanding the earnest efforts, in language more forcible than pious, of their commander, Major Reynolds,

---

[6] H.T.I. letter. Also, "...the 27th was ordered to join in a general assault, and went in with other regiments bravely, driving the rebels back to the cover of the masked batteries." Rochester *Union and Advertiser*, July 29, 1861; a column, composed of the Twenty-seventh New York, Eleventh and Fifth Massachusetts, First Minnesota, and Sixty-ninth New York, moved up toward the left flank of the batteries." *O.R..*, Vol. 2, 385. Note, a portion of the 69th was in zouaves uniforms, and Porter could have mistaken them for the 11th New York zouaves.
[7] *O.R..*, Vol. 2, 403.

broke and ran to the rear, soon followed by the unsupported Fourteenth.[8]

Heintzelman, as we stated, was critical of the 14th for this action. Additionally, several members of the 38th also wrote home describing the 14th's actions in unflattering terms – "they ran like sheep down the hill."[9] What these observers did not realize was this was the third major engagement for the 14th thus far in the battle. They were previously shaken from their action on Matthew's Hill. Then they were driven off Henry Hill, along with the other troops, only to be advanced into the fray again. It is a credit to the officers and men of the regiment that they were able to rally and advance this time at all.

Now, further to the left, Colonel Sherman's brigade was also becoming involved in the effort to take Henry Hill. As described earlier, his 13th New York had advanced up the slope, but was driven off to another elevation to the left. The remainder of the brigade sought cover behind the slight embankment along the Warrenton Road, waiting for orders to advance.

Although the regiments were not far from the hill, a member of the 79th wrote:

> [We] were unable to witness all that had just transpired [Griffin's guns being overrun]; the depression of the roadway prevented our seeing, and also saved us from musketry fire of the enemy, but shells from their batteries in the rear of the Henry house dropped into the road, killing and wounding some and making us feel nervous and excited.[10]

While in the road, Sherman recalled, "by order of Major Wadsworth, of General McDowell's staff, I ordered [the brigade] to leave the roadway by the left flank, and attack the enemy."

---

[8] *History of the Fighting Fourteenth*, 230. Again, it is important to remember that although these men were called Marines, they were merely raw recruits thrown into a Marine battalion.

[9] Capt. W.H. Baird letter, July 23, 1861 and John. H. Morrison letter, July 23, 1861.

[10] Todd, *Seventy-Ninth Highlanders*, 37.

Sherman called for the 2nd Wisconsin to exit the road, form their ranks, and attack up the slope.[11]

Unfortunately, Sherman made the mistake of sending his brigade in piecemeal, rather than as a unified group. The realities of his command, very large regiments filled with raw recruits, probably swayed his decision to do this. Leading a coordinated effort up the hill with over 3,000 new enlistees would have been extremely difficult. Thus, realities probably dictated his sending in one regiment at a time, whose progress could be monitored and then reinforcements could be sent where needed.

The 2nd Wisconsin marched up the north slope, past the Robinson house and on toward the Henry house. They met a staggering fire on the top from Jackson's men, partially supported by members of Hampton's Legion. The uniforms of the 2nd Wisconsin caused problems for the Confederates, however, for they wore gray. But once their identity was confirmed, they received a withering fire.[12]

Once the ranks of the 2nd Wisconsin were depleted, they fell back down the hill. Seeing this, Colonel Sherman ordered up his next regiment, the 79th New York Highlanders, led by Colonel James Cameron.

Back when the 79th originally formed and elected officers, the position of colonel was vacant. While at a party in Washington in early June, officers of the 79th met Secretary of War Simon Cameron. The Secretary suggested that if the officers were to elect his brother, James, as colonel, he would accept the position. They met and decided upon Cameron. Hearing of his election, he accepted the honor on June 21st. A factor helping his chances of being accepted was the rumor that Cameron was a descendant of an "old Scottish Chieftain."[13]

Although their commander's brother was the Secretary of War, the men of the 79th soon found that this would not necessarily guarantee them special treatment. When still encamped in Washington, they marched to an arsenal, fully expecting to trade in their antiquated flintlock converted muskets for rifled muskets – which were promised. Arriving at the arsenal, they were instead

---

[11] *O.R..*, Vol. 2, 369.
[12] Davis, *Battle at Bull Run*, 217; *O.R..*, Vol. 2, 369.
[13] Todd, *Seventy-Ninth Highlanders*, 13-14.

was not to be a victim that day, and the conviction made me feel perfectly calm.[16]

With the 79th falling back, it was now time for the 69th to take their turn. The Irishmen formed ranks and started up the slope. Now, however, the 69th faced a new problem. Many members of the 79th, in a disorganized state, were impeding the 69th's advance. "[O]ur regiment formed into line directly in front of the enemy's battery," wrote an officer in the 69th, "charged upon it twice, were driven off, owing principally to the panic of the regiment which preceded us..."[17]

The particulars of the 69th's attack are not well documented, but the following account comes from the brigade's history:

> [Captain Thomas F.] Meagher's company of Zouaves [in the 69th] suffered desperately, their red dress making them a conspicuous mark for the enemy. When Meagher's horse was torn from under him by a rifled cannon ball, he jumped up, waved his sword, and exclaimed, "Boys! Look at that flag – remember Ireland and Fontenoy." The regiment bravely but vainly struggled to capture the batteries, and drive the enemy from the shelter of the wood.[18]

Thomas Meagher was an Irish revolutionary who had been arrested in Ireland, by the British, and exiled to "Australia, to undergo his penal servitude." He managed to escape and made his way to the U.S., where he established a law practice in New York City. Here, he became famous for his writings and Irish nationalism. At the outbreak of the war he was a captain of a company in the 69th, whom he led into battle.[19]

While Sherman's troops were taking their turn advancing, being repulsed, and then retiring, fresh troops were arriving on

---

[16] Narrative about two men captured at Bull Run. *Ibid.*, 51-52.

[17] 69th's report, *O.R..*, Vol. 2, 372.

[18] Conyngham, *The Irish Brigade*, 37. Most of the regiment was dressed in regulation blue uniforms, but Meagher's company was outfitted in zouave uniforms.

[19] *Ibid.*, 535-536.

Charge of the 79th New York. Colonel James Cameron shown at the right.
Drawing from William Todd's *Seventy-Ninth Highlanders*

both sides. Colonel Oliver Howard led his brigade into action further to the Federal right. In the meantime, Beauregard was also receiving fresh regiments.

At this point, the tide of battle was about go against the Federals. As the hour of 4:00 was fast approaching, McDowell's forces were making their last desperate efforts to claim the hill and the abandoned guns.

Chapter Ten

"There Was a Chance

to Try Men"

McDowell and his subordinates were busy rounding up regiments or parts of commands, pointing them at the hill and sending them up the slope. They in turn were repulsed, and usually came tumbling back. Soon another went to take their place. Finally, as the climax of the battle was at hand, the 13th New York was again summoned to make an attack up the hill.

Before their advance, the regiment was still on or near the elevation it earlier occupied, and was apparently supporting a battery. In a letter home to his mother after the battle, an officer of the 13th described the action.

> The 13th Regiment have covered themselves with glory. We were ordered to support Carlisle's battery, that was playing on a tremendous masked battery, on the summit of a high hill. We lay for two hours on our faces, and had our men torn to pieces by the shell and grape shot, that came into us, as fast as 20 or 30 cannon could pour it in. Our battery being all torn to pieces, we were ordered to charge the enemy, who were on the top of the hill. There was a chance to try men.[1]

---

[1] Henry B. Williams letter, July 24, 1861.

This charge, as with most of the earlier efforts, was surrounded in confusion. Members of the 13th wrote:

> Already as we advanced our regiment as well as the 69th and 79th, had become completely dissolved, and I met here [on top of the hill] men from all companies, posted partly behind the house, partly behind the fence, and firing upon the enemy, whose cannon balls and musket and rifle bullets were continually whizzing round our heads.[2]

> We were called for, and our gallant regiment *took the lead*, and surrounded them [a group of Confederates on the hill], whilst the other regiments followed, and then the tug commenced. The bullets flew thicker than dust, and while poor fellows were falling on every side, thank God! I came out safe, without even a wound of any kind. My bayonet was shot off close to my side, and my blanket riddled with balls. Our red blankets formed a good target to shoot at.[3]

> Sergeant Daniel Sharp, Color Bearer, ran to the front of the regiment several feet, and while the balls were (using his own language) "Playing Yankee Doodle about his head," whirled the Stars and Stripes in the face of the enemy, cooling turning around and taking his place again in the ranks.[4]

> We next made a charge at a house close to the masked batteries, where they were shielded by bushes and trees. Here we stood fifteen minutes under a galling fire, our poor fellows dropping like falling leaves. We were told to stop firing, as those in the house were our troops. The infamous rebels displayed the American flag there to deceive and get the advantage of us.[5]

---

[2] Anonymous, German soldier. July 23, 1861.
[3] Thomas Dukelow letter.
[4] A.G.C. letter, July 30, 1861.
[5] William Fleming letter, July 24, 1861.

The displaying of the American flag was an event echoed by other members of the regiment.[6] In actuality, rather than a rouse, it was probably a case of mistaken identity. The first Confederate flag looked remarkably like the stars and stripes at a distance and in the smoke. Several other regiments claimed seeing this same type of thing – as we saw with the 79th New York Highlanders. In fact, following the battle, the Southern troops began carrying the now famous Confederate battle flag, modeled after the Saint Andrew's cross.[7]

When the men of the 13th ceased firing, trying to figure out if they were facing friend or foe, a new problem developed.

> Such was the confusion thus induced [by seeing the 'American flag' and the 13th ceasing fire] that our own troops commenced firing into us, supposing we were the enemy, killing several. This, together with a galling fire from the enemy's masked batteries and muskets, compelled us to retreat…"[8]

The troops firing on them were, apparently, the 69th and possibly some remaining members of the 79th. Contrary to the above testimony, others claimed this fire did little or no harm, but it greatly shook the men and they began to retire.[9]

While these events were playing out on the left, far off to the right, toward Howard's position, a very important development would precipitate the end of the battle. Beauregard and Johnston's fresh troops were rolling into line on the Confederate left. Thus, Howard's troops, exhausted from their march to the front, faced increasing numbers of Southern forces. Before long some of Howard's troops began streaming for the rear, followed by others.

---

[6] Ensign Gilbert letter, July 27, 1861; Henry B. Williams letter, July 24, 1861; Sam Partridge letter, July 24, 1861; *Rochester in the Civil War*, 80.

[7] McPherson, *Battle Cry of Freedom*, 342.

[8] William Fleming letter, July 24, 1861.

[9] Henry B. Williams letter, July 24, 1861; A.G.C. letter, July 30, 1861. "A.G.C." He wrote that a member of the 69th later admitted some men in the 69th fired in their direction on purpose. He claimed that because they stopped firing they wanted them out of the way. He also hinted at a rivalry developing between the two regiments for the 'position of honor.'

Soon a panic was created on McDowell's right as Union troops began running. Seeing these troops retiring in panic did nothing to help the resolve of those Federal troops who had been fighting most of the day on the left.

With the right flank dissolving, the commanders ordered the regiments attacking Henry Hill back. At first most units retired in good order, preparing to make a stand again near the Matthew's Hill, but soon panic spread all along the line.

The retreat on the Federal right helped precipitate a panic throughout the field for two reasons. First, it weakened the resolve of the other Union troops that were trying to make a stand. Additionally, it greatly inspired the Confederate troops to press their attack even harder.

Soon, as the withdrawing forces neared Bull Run, fear spread. A well-aimed shell crashed into a wagon and blocked the Stone Bridge. Further congesting the route of escape was the presence of the civilians who had come to watch the battle. Among these was Congressman Alfred Ely, who was captured and held by the Confederates.

A New York soldier described how the retreat turned to panic.

> Before we entered the woods, the cry arose that the cavalry were upon us, and such a scramble I never saw. The officers ordered the men to the cover to save themselves. Baggage-wagons, artillery, ambulances and carriages of every description thundered on by us, and the whole route was strewn with broken wagons, or deserted ones filled with provisions, munitions and all the appurtenances of war, besides large amounts of private property belonging to the officers.[10]

Although many Federals, including some New York units, made a brave stand near Centerville and then many retreated in order, the majority of Union troops ran for the safety of the Capital, leaving their weapons and accoutrements behind. The battle at Bull Run was decided; the Federals were defeated.

---

[10] J.A. Copeland letter, July 24, 1861.

Chapter Eleven

"This Rout Beats Anything"

As the Federals troops scrambled back to Washington, many a soldier took pen in hand, trying to give words to the incredible things they had experienced.

The carnage in the battle was awful and the sights beyond description. The heavy booming of cannon, the rapid volleys of musketry, the shrieks of the wounded, the piles of dead and dying men and horses – were dreadful. Those who were there, and who have been in the Mexican and Crimean wars, on the heights of Solferino and Magenta, say that such another battle, under equal circumstances, never was known.[1]

You have seen pictures [drawings and paintings] of battles, but they can convey no idea of what battle is....[I]magine thousands of men gathered over several square miles of ground, in valleys, in ravines, in the beds of streams, on hills, behind rocks, in the woods, everywhere, killing each other, and you may have some idea of where I was Sunday. It was not a battle, it was a regular slaughter.[2]

I shall long remember that battle-field as long as I live. Such sights as I saw there! It makes me shudder to think

---

[1] A.B.M. letter, July 24, 1861.
[2] S.A.M. letter, July 23, 1861.

now, but then I did not think of anything but to fire at every traitor I could see.[3]

This is probably one of the hardest fought battles we have ever had in America, and this rout beats anything ever read of in any history.[4]

Along with these stories, they also tried to make sense of why they lost. Some blamed their commander.

We think that our General (McDowell) commenced operations too soon.... Gen. McDowell probably thought that if he could win the fight with so few men the honor and glory would be greater for him; when, if he had waited 24 hours longer, we should have put to flight every soldier in the Southern army.[5]

Rumors spread that General McDowell was glory hunting and tried to fight the entire rebel force without waiting for Patterson's army to join him. They did not understand the reason McDowell had to fight both Johnston's and Beaurgard's forces was because Patterson did not do what was asked of him, to occupy Johnston and keep him from moving toward Manassas.

Along with the disappointment of defeat, these ninety-day recruits, many of whom stated they would not sign on for longer than their initial enlistment *before* Bull Run, now heard some unpleasant news – the governor of New York had turned them over to the Federal government for the remainder of their two year terms. For many, this was very disheartening. One soldier sent off a note to his local newspaper.

---

[3] H.T.I. letter.

[4] J.A. Copeland letter, July 24, 1861.

[5] C.W.M. letter, July 24, 1861. Another soldier wrote that Patterson's forces were supposed to arrive "Monday, the day the battle was to have been fought; but Gen. McDowell, contrary to orders from Gen. Scott not to attack with his own force alone, began the battle..." C.B. letter, July 24, 1861.

Mr. Editor: – It is generally known that our time of enlistment of these three months expired last Tuesday, and
that we are still held here and are kicked and nosed about
like dogs.[6]

A member of the 13th New York later wrote of the event in
his own brief his history of the unit.

Immediate discharge and return home was expected,
and expectation appeared to be made certain, by the arrival, at this particular junction of orders to that effect from
the war department. Disappoint followed, and it was severe. The men could hardly believe that Governor
Morgan had turned them over, as it was termed, for the
two years to the general government, yet such was the
fact. Dissatisfaction followed in which it might be said all
joined. It was so deep and general that the most serious
consequences were apprehended. Thirty were sent to the
Dry Tortugas rather than stay, as they said, for a term for
which they had not engaged.[7]

Although most were not pleased with the way they were
forced into extended service, the majority served loyally. Many of
these units fought in many campaigns over the next two years.

Of the thirty-four regiments that crossed Bull Run and were
engaged in battle on July 21, 1861, nearly one-third were from
New York – eleven regiments. This tally is as large as the next
three largest states combined. Thus, New York contributed more
toward this Union effort than any other state.

This was the case throughout the war; New York supplied
more men and suffered more casualties in the Civil War than any
other Northern state. Unfortunately, it would take nearly four more
years to end the clash and many other battles that eclipsed what
was then known as "The greatest battle of the age."

---

[6] "A Private" letter, August 17, 1861.
[7] Cazeau, *Account of the Thirteenth New York*, 2.

Appendix One

Order of Battle

Brigadier General Irwin McDowell's Army

Brig. Gen. Daniel Tyler's First Division

Col. E.D. Keyes 1st Brigade
2nd Maine
1st Connecticut
2nd Connecticut
3rd Connecticut

Brig. Gen. R.C. Schenck 2nd Brigade
2nd New York State Militia
1st Ohio
2nd Ohio
Battery E, 2nd U.S. Artillery

Col. William T. Sherman 3rd Brigade
13th New York Volunteers
69th New York State Militia
79th New York State Militia
2nd Wisconsin
Battery E, 3rd U.S. Artillery

Col. I.B. Richardson, 4th Brigade
1st Mass.
12th New York Volunteers
2nd Michigan
3rd Michigan

Battery G, 1st U.S. Artillery
Battery M, 2nd U.S. Artillery

Col. David Hunter (wounded) Second Division (replaced by Col. Porter)

Col. Andrew Porter 1st Brigade
8th New York State Militia
14th New York State Militia (14th Brooklyn)
27th New York Volunteers
Battalion U.S. Infantry
Battalion U.S. Marines
Battalion U.S. Cavalry
Battery D, 5th U.S. Artillery

Col. A.E. Burnside 2nd Brigade
2nd New Hampshire
1st Rhode Island
2nd Rhode Island
71st New York State Militia – including two howitzers
Rhode Island Artillery

Col. S. P. Heintzelman, Third Division

Col. W. B. Franklin, 1st Brigade
5th Massachusetts
11th Massachusetts
1st Minnesota
Battery I, First U.S. Artillery

Col. O. B. Willcox, Second Brigade
11th New York Volunteers (Fire Zouaves)
38th New York Volunteers
1st Michigan
4th Michigan
Battery D, 2nd U.S. Artillery

Col. O. O. Howard, Third Brigade
3rd Maine
4th Maine

5th Maine
2nd Vermont

Appendix Two

Where were they from?

Counties and Mustering Points

Allegany County - Angelica
27th New York Volunteers – Co. I.
Brooklyn
14th New York State Militia (14th Brooklyn)
Broome County - Binghamton
27th New York Volunteers – Cos. C, D, and F.
Chemung County - Horseheads
38th New York Volunteers – Co. I.
Cortland County - Homer
12th New York Volunteers – Co. D.
Dutchess County
38th New York Volunteers – Co. G.
Essex County - Elizabethtown
38th New York Volunteers – Co. K.
Genesee County - Batavia
12th New York Volunteers – Co. K.
Livingston County
 - Dansville
13th New York Volunteers – Co. B.
 - Lima
27th New York Volunteers – Co. G.
 - Mount Morris
27th New York Volunteers – Co. H.
Madison County - Canastota
12th New York Volunteers – Co. G.

Monroe County
- Brockport
>13th New York Volunteers – Co. K.
- Rochester
>13th New York Volunteers – Cos. A, C, D, E, F, G, H and I.
>27th New York Volunteers – Co. E.

New York City
>2nd New York State Militia
>8th New York State Militia
>11th New York Volunteers
>38th New York Volunteers – Cos. A, B, C, D, and F.
>69th New York State Militia
>71st New York State Militia
>79th New York State Militia

Onondaga County
- Liverpool
>12th New York Volunteers – Co. F.
- Syracuse
>12th New York Volunteers – Cos. A, B, C, E, H, and I.

Ontario County - Geneva
>38th New York Volunteers – Co. H.

Orleans County - Albion
>27th New York Volunteers – Co. K.

Wayne County - Lyons
>27th New York Volunteers – Co. B.

Westchester County
>38th New York Volunteers – Co. E and G.

White Plains
>27th New York Volunteers – Co. A

Bibliography

Letters:

A.D.A. letter, May 24, 1861. Benedum Books newspaper archive.

A.D.A. "Punishing a Renegade" letter, May 24, 1861. Benedum Books newspaper archive.

A.D.A. letter. Benedum Books newspaper archive.

E.A. letter. Benedum Books newspaper archive.

S. C. Anderson testimony at the Court of inquiry concerning Captain Locke's conduct during the fight on   July 18.

Anonymous, "An Episode" letter, June 15, 1861. Benedum Books newspaper archive.

Anonymous: "Another Private" letter. Benedum Books newspaper archive.

Anonymous: German soldier. July 23, 1861. Originally in the German language newspaper *Genesee Observer*, Benedum Books newspaper archive.

"B." letter, June 10, 1861. Benedum Books newspaper archive.

Capt. W.H. Baird letter, July 23, 1861. Benedum Books newspaper archive.

Daniel W. Bosley letter, July 25, 1861. Benedum Books newspaper archive.

C.B. letter, July 24, 1861. Benedum Books newspaper archive.

C.T.B. letter, June 3, 1861. Benedum Books newspaper archive.

E.C.B. letter, July 30, 1861. Reprinted in the Syracuse *Courier and Union*, August 6, 1861.

Captain H. A. Barnum letter to the Syracuse *Standard.* (date unclear).

William H. Benjamin account. Benedum Books newspaper archive.

Daniel W. Bosley letter, July 25, 1861. Benedum Books newspaper archive.

T. L. Bowman letter to his father. Benedum Books newspaper archive.

T. L. Bowman account. Benedum Books newspaper archive.

Lucinda Briscoll letter, May 31, 1861. Benedum Books newspaper archive.

Byles Jr. letter, May 27, 1861. Benedum Books newspaper archive.

A.G.C. letter, May 10, 1861. Benedum Books newspaper archive.

A.G.C. letter, June 3, 1861. Benedum Books newspaper archive.

A.G.C. letter, June 17, 1861. Benedum Books newspaper archive.

A.G.C. letter, July 7, 1861. Benedum Books newspaper archive.

A.G.C. letter, July 20, 1861. Benedum Books newspaper archive.

A.G.C. letter, July 30, 1861. Benedum Books newspaper archive.

"Carrie" letter, June 29, 1861. Benedum Books newspaper archive.

"Carrie" letter, July 18, 1861. Benedum Books newspaper archive.
Giles Cheseborough testimony at the Court of inquiry concerning
    Captain Locke's conduct during the fight on July 18.

William Clague letter, July 23, 1861. Benedum Books newspaper
    archive.

J.A. Copeland letter, July 24, 1861. Benedum Books newspaper archive.

Thomas Dukelow letter. Benedum Books newspaper archive.

C.P.D. letter, July 7, 1861. Benedum Books newspaper archive.

C.P.D. letter, July 13, 1861. Benedum Books newspaper archive.

C.E.E. letter, May 9, 1861. Benedum Books newspaper archive.

C.E.E. letter, May 19, 1861. Benedum Books newspaper archive.

C.E.E. letter (?), May 28, 1861. Benedum Books newspaper archive.

C.E.E. letter, June 5, 1861. Benedum Books newspaper archive.

C.E.E. letter, June 28, 1861. Benedum Books newspaper archive.

"Ed" letter, July 19, 1861. Benedum Books newspaper archive.

"Ensign" letter. May 8, 1861. Benedum Books newspaper archive.

"Ensign" letter. June 15, 1861. Benedum Books newspaper archive.

"Ensign" letter. June 19, 1861. Benedum Books newspaper archive.

"Ensign" letter. June 22, 1861. Benedum Books newspaper archive.

"Ensign" letter. Benedum Books newspaper archive.

Walter Fleming letter, June 4, 1861. Benedum Books newspaper archive.

Walter Fleming letter, July 5, 1861. Benedum Books newspaper archive.

Walter Fleming letter, July 22, 1861. Benedum Books newspaper archive.

Walter Fleming letter, July 23, 1861. Benedum Books newspaper archive.

William Fleming letter, June 26, 1861. Benedum Books newspaper archive.

William Fleming letter, July 24, 1861. Benedum Books newspaper archive.

Edward French letter to his wife. Benedum Books newspaper archive.

"Friend C." letter, June 24, 1861. Benedum Books newspaper archive.

"Friend E." letter, June 23, 1861. Benedum Books newspaper archive.

J.C.G. letter, May 15, 1861. Benedum Books newspaper archive.

Frank Gates letter, July 23, 1861. Syracuse *Courier and Union*, (date unclear).

B. Gilbert letter to his brother, June 21, 1861. Syracuse *Daily Journal*, June 17, 1861.

Ensign Gilbert letter, July 27, 1861. Benedum Books newspaper archive.

Edward Gould letter, July 24, 1861. Benedum Books newspaper archive.

"Grumbler" letter, June 4, 1861. Benedum Books newspaper archive.

"H" letter, June 24, 1861. Benedum Books newspaper archive.

"Haversack" letter, July 9, 1861. Benedum Books newspaper archive.

H.T.I. letter. Benedum Books newspaper archive.

"Illinois" letter, June 10, 1861. Benedum Books newspaper archive.

R. J. letter, June 22, 1861. Benedum Books newspaper archive.

"Knapsack" letter, May 7, 1861. Benedum Books newspaper archive.

R.D.L. letter, May 14, 1861. Benedum Books newspaper archive.

R.D.L. letter, May 22, 1861. Benedum Books newspaper archive.

Major John Lewis letter, May 31, 1861. Syracuse *Daily Journal*, June 14, 1861.

A.B.M. letter, July 24, 1861. Benedum Books newspaper archive.

C.W.M. letter, May 9, 1861. Benedum Books newspaper archive.

C.W.M. letter, July 24, 1861. Benedum Books newspaper archive.

J.D.M. letter. Benedum Books newspaper archive.

J.D.Mc. letter, May 14, 1861. Benedum Books newspaper archive.

P.M. letter. Benedum Books newspaper archive.

S.A.M. letter, May 22, 1861. Benedum Books newspaper archive.

S.A.M. letter, May 25, 1861. Benedum Books newspaper archive.

S.A.M. letter, May 31, 1861. Benedum Books newspaper archive.

S.A.M. letter, June 7, 1861. Benedum Books newspaper archive.

S.A.M. letter, July 23, 1861. Benedum Books newspaper archive.

Mac letter, June 2, 1861. Benedum Books newspaper archive.

Mac letter, June 30, 1861. Benedum Books newspaper archive.

Mack letter, June 27, 1861. Benedum Books newspaper archive.

George Matthews letter, July 27, 1861. Benedum Books newspaper archive.

Homer Merrill letter, July 27, 1861. Benedum Books newspaper archive.

John H. Morrison letter, July 15, 1861. Benedum Books newspaper archive.

John H. Morrison letter, July 23, 1861. Benedum Books newspaper archive.

Asamel Morse letter, July 23, 1861. Benedum Books newspaper archive.

Daniel Page letter to his father. Benedum Books newspaper archive.

R.W. Pease letter. Syracuse *Courier and Union*, August 6, 1861.

William Petton testimony at the Court of inquiry concerning Captain Locke's conduct during the fight on July 18. Reprinted in the Syracuse *Courier and Union*, August 14, 1861.

"A Private" letter, August 17, 1861. Syracuse *Courier and Union*, August 20, 1861.

"A Private's letter." Benedum Books newspaper archive.

Col. Isaac Quinby letter, June 17, 1861. Benedum Books newspaper archive.

George W. Rowe letter, July 19, 1861. Clipping from 12th N.Y. folder at the Onondaga County Historical Society. (12th N.Y.)

George L. Russell letter, July 23, 1861. Benedum Books newspaper archive.

"S" letter, June 4, 1861. Benedum Books newspaper archive.

J.S. letter, June 15, 1861. Benedum Books newspaper archive.

J.S. letter, June 24, 1861. Benedum Books newspaper archive.

J.W.S. letter. Benedum Books newspaper archive.

Capt. Schoeffel letter, July 7, 1861. Benedum Books newspaper archive.

"Skirmisher" letter, July 26, 1861 (12th New York). (Syracuse newspaper reprint, but paper and date unclear.)

W.H. Swan letter, (post Bull Run). Benedum Books newspaper archive.

A.W.T. letter, June 30, 1861. Benedum Books newspaper archive.

A.W.T. letter, July 4, 1861. Benedum Books newspaper archive.

A.W.T. letter, July 13, 1861. Benedum Books newspaper archive.

A.W.T. letter, July 18, 1861. Benedum Books newspaper archive.

O.L. Terry letter, June 16, 1861. Benedum Books newspaper archive.

G.W.W. letter. Benedum Books newspaper archive.

H.H.W. letter, July 19, 1861. Benedum Books newspaper archive.

J.G.W. letter, July 20, 1861. Benedum Books newspaper archive.

M.R.W. letter, July 18, 1861. Benedum Books newspaper archive.

Col. E. L. Walrath letter to Mayor Andrews, June 8, 1861. Syracuse *Daily Journal*, June 14, 1861.

Col. E. L. Walrath letter, July 12, 1861. Syracuse *Courier and Union*, July 12, 1861.

Col. E. L. Walrath letter, July 28, 1861. Syracuse *Courier and Union,* July 31, 1861.

Walter letter, June 4, 1861. Benedum Books newspaper archive.

G. Wiley Wells letter, July 23, 1861. Benedum Books newspaper archive.

H.B. Williams letter, July 19, 1861. Benedum Books newspaper archive.

Henry B. Williams letter, July 24, 1861. Benedum Books newspaper archive.

Ira Wood letter, July 23, 1861. Reprinted in a contemporary Onondaga County Newspaper.

E. P. Woodford letter. Newspaper clipping from Onondaga Historical Society "12th New York Volunteers" folder.

Books and Articles:

Bilby, Joseph G. *Remember Fontenoy! The 69th New York and the Irish Brigade in the Civil War*. Longstreet House, Hightstown, N.J.: 1995.

Cazeau, Theodore. *A Brief Account of the Thirteenth New York State Volunteer Regiment, 1861-1863*. N.P., Circa 1920.

"Chronology of Important Events Connected with the 12th N. Y. S. Volunteers." 12th N. Y. S. folder, Onondaga County Historical Society.

Conyngham, D. P. *The Irish Brigade and Its Campaigns*. New York: 1867.

"Court of Inquiry" Report: General Orders Number 30, August 12, 1861. File folder for the 12th New York at the Onondaga Historical Society.

Davis, William C. *Battle at Bull Run: A History of the First Major Campaign of the Civil War*. Stackpole Books reprint, original copyright 1977.

Davis, William C. and the editors of Time-Life. *First Blood: Fort Sumter to Bull Run*. Time-Life Books: 1983.

Esposito, Vincent J. *The West Point Atlas of Americans Wars*. Vol I. 1699-1900. Frederick A. Praeger, Publishers: New York, 1959.

Fairchild, C. B. *History of the 27th Regiment N. Y. Vols*. 1888, Binghamton, N.Y.

Fox, William F. *New York at Gettysburg*, 3 Vols. J.B. Lyon and Co., Albany, N.Y.: 1900.

Johnston, Jr. Terry A. ed. *"Him on One Side and Me on the Other" The Civil War Letters of Alexander Campbell, 79th New York Infantry Regiment and James Campbell, 1st South Carolina Battalion*. University of South Carolina: 1999.

"Leaves From an Officer's Diary – The 12th New York Regiment of Volunteers at Blackburn's Ford." Syracuse *Courier and Union*, November 11, 1880.

Mathless, Paul, ed. *Voices of the Civil War: First Manassas*. Time-Life Books, New York: 1997.

McKay, Ernest A. *The Civil War and New York City*. Syracuse University Press: 1990.

McKelvey, Blake. Ed. *Rochester in the Civil War*. Rochester Historical Society Publications, Rochester, N.Y.: 1944.

McKnight, W. Mark. *Blue Bonnets O'er the Border: The 79th New York Cameron Highlanders*. White Maine Books, Shippensburg, Pa.: 1998.

McPherson, James A. *Battle Cry of Freedom.* Oxford University Press: 1988.

Metcalf, Lewis H. "So Eager Were We All…" *American Heritage*, June 1965, pages 32-41.

"Military Intelligence: Pay, Clothing and Rations" *Clyde Times Semi-weekly*, May 15, 1861.

Nevins, Allan. *The War For the Union: The Improvised War.* Charles Scribner's Sons, New York: 1959.

"The Onondaga Regiment" Syracuse *Daily Journal*, May 4, 1861.

"An Officer of the Army" letter. Originally printed in *New York Times*, reprinted in *Clyde Times Semiweekly*, July 17, 1861.

"Rochester for the Union!" Rochester *Union and Advertiser*, April 17, 1861.

Sherman, William T. *Memoirs of William T Sherman.* 2 Vols. New York: 1875.

Todd, William. *The Seventy-Ninth Highlanders: New York Volunteers in the War of Rebellion.* Brandow, Barton and Co., Albany, N.Y.: 1886.

Townsend, Thomas S. *Honors of the Empire State in the War of the Rebellion.* New York: 1889.

Trevis, C. V. *The History of the Fighting Fourteenth* [Brooklyn]. New York: Brooklyn Eagle Press, 1911.

Ward, Geoffrey C. *The Civil War: An Illustrated History.* Alfred A. Knopf, Inc., New York: 1990.

"The War Begun – The Rebels Bombard Fort Sumter" Rochester *Union and Advertiser*, April 13, 1861.

War of the Rebellion: Official Records of the Union and Confederate Armies. Part I, 128 Vols. Government Printing Office, Washington: 1880.

"Wayne County in the Field" *Clyde Times Semiweekly*, May 8, 1861.

Index